The Pricing Journey

The Pricing Journey

THE ORGANIZATIONAL TRANSFORMATION TOWARD PRICING EXCELLENCE

Stephan M. Liozu

STANFORD BUSINESS BOOKS

An Imprint of Stanford University Press

Stanford, California

Stanford University Press
Stanford, California

Special discounts for bulk quantities of Stanford Business Books are available to
corporations, professional associations, and other organizations. For details and
discount information, contact the special sales department of Stanford University
Press. Tel: (650) 736-1782, Fax: (650) 736-1784

Printed in the United States of America on acid-free, archival-quality paper

Library of Congress Cataloging-in-Publication Data

Liozu, Stephan, author.
   The pricing journey : the organizational transformation toward pricing
excellence / Stephan M. Liozu.
      pages cm
   Includes bibliographical references and index.
   ISBN 978-0-8047-8874-8 (cloth : alk. paper)
   1. Pricing.   2. Organizational change.   I. Title.
   HF5416.5.L557 2015
   658.8'16—dc23

                                                                    2014042784

Typeset by Newgen in 10.5/15 Minion

To my son, Lorenzo,
the love of my life.
May this work give him inspiration
to go beyond the possible
and to discover his own journey in life!

Contents

Foreword

In Economics 101, we learn that prices move quickly in response to supply and demand. Pricing researchers, however, know better. With some exceptions, pricing is almost never that fluid. Most prices tend to be sticky, in ways that often work against the seller (Bergen et al. 2003). More perplexing still, pricing structures can persist in a market for decades even when it is clear that they hurt both buyers and sellers.

Three examples illustrate this fact. The first concerns gasoline prices on European motorways. On-highway gasoline is more expensive than gasoline on smaller roads because petrol companies bid and pay for the right to operate stations on highways. Given their own higher operating costs, these companies sell petrol on highways at a 5 to 8 percent premium. Many customers have become aware of this discrepancy. As a result, some petrol stations have seen their sales volume drop by 80 to 90 percent over the last few years, although traffic volume has risen in many places. Reliably high motorway prices have taught customers to fill the tanks of their fuel-efficient cars before long trips and to avoid on-highway petrol stations. In this situation, the only rational pricing strategy would be to set prices to match off-highway levels and capture profits through the sale of other items (snacks, coffee, etc.). But this is not what we see. Prices stay high, and rather than change their pricing structure and recapture their market share, many service station operators on the highway are considering shutting down. A choice that may have made sense when cars were less efficient and customers didn't really have a choice but to stop persists even now, although both buyers and sellers are painfully aware of how dysfunctional this is.

This happens in business-to-business pricing too. In online databases, for instance, time-based access pricing, a rather arbitrary choice made in the early days of the 1970s, became the predominant way to price access to online databases and stayed that way for decades (Farjoun 2002). Time-based pricing does not reflect the value that customers derive from access to information and penalizes less technologically savvy customers (who may take more time to find information). Yet pricing based on access time remained the predominant approach to pricing database use long after nearly all participants—publishers, producers, vendors, and customers—had recognized its deficiencies. Only in the 1990s, when upstarts entered the market, did the pricing structure evolve toward approaches that better reflect the value to customers: subscription-based models and flat fees.

Professional services are also often trapped by outmoded pricing modes. Lawyers, consultants, and physicians implicitly know that the primary value of their services resides in the output customers achieve as a result of their intervention (e.g., a victory in court, a performance improvement, or a behavioral change, respectively), yet providers of intellectual services still price their services primarily based on their own time (days/hours), regardless of the value they deliver. Here too, the primary actors probably recognize that time-based billing is dysfunctional (leading randomly to prices that are either too high or too low and almost never aligned with value), yet time-based pricing remains the dominant pricing approach for nearly all providers of intellectual services.

These three examples all illuminate the deficiencies of cost-based pricing approaches. But these three examples also illustrate that arbitrary decisions can persist for decades even though both parties involved—sellers and buyers—have long recognized their dysfunctionality. So far, we largely lack a robust theory explaining the persistence of outdated pricing practices. To be sure, academic researchers know very well that value-based pricing, unlike cost-based pricing, aligns the interest of firms and customers, thus leading to superior firm profitability. However, academic researchers have assumed that the transition from cost-based pricing to value-based pricing is relatively straightforward.

Not so to Stephan Liozu. In this book, Liozu takes a nuanced view and shows that implementation of value-based pricing is an act of organizational transformation that requires new capabilities, new structures, new incentives, and, above all, a deep-seated confidence that the company can adapt to an unfamiliar value system.

Liozu emphasizes the role of change management in achieving better pricing. He finds that the ability of an organization to achieve better prices requires it to internalize new behaviors—including new methods for pricing and selling—and that teaching and enforcing these behaviors depends on the cooperation of midlevel pricing managers, senior executives, and most importantly, an active, engaged chief executive officer (CEO). Pricing, Liozu argues, is fundamentally a strategic tool: Strategic, since pricing is an integral part of firm strategy. Strategic also because pricing meets the definition of competitive advantage, since it is valuable, rare, difficult to imitate, nonsubstitutable, and embedded in the firm's organization (Barney 1991).

Pricing, Liozu argues, can and should become a strategic activity, because new pricing approaches frequently disrupt industries, usually to the advantage of the initiating company. Consider GE's "power by the hour" turbine leases, salesforce.com's software-as-a-service pricing, Zipcar's by-the-minute pricing of rental cats, or Monsanto's value-based pricing for genetically modified seeds; they all illustrate how changes in pricing structure can constitute breakthroughs that raise profits and customer satisfaction at the same time. Now, for the first time, Liozu demonstrates that such innovations are not simply a matter of intuition and luck but the result of superior management, discipline, and creativity.

I am confident that *The Pricing Journey* will be a valuable resource for executives who want to fundamentally reshape pricing structures to their own and, ultimately, to their customers' advantage.

Andreas Hinterhuber, PhD
Hinterhuber & Partners
Innsbruck, Austria
February 2015

References

Barney, J. B. 1991. "Firm Resources and Sustained Competitive Advantage." *Journal of Management* 17 (1): 99–120.

Bergen, M., M. Ritson, S. Dutta, D. Levy, and M. Zbaracki. 2003. "Shattering the Myth of Costless Price Changes." *European Management Journal* 21 (6): 663–669.

Farjoun, M. 2002. "The Dialectics of Institutional Development in Emerging and Turbulent Fields: The History of Pricing Conventions in the On-Line Database Industry." *Academy of Management Journal* 45 (5): 848–874.

Acknowledgments

The last four years have been a real journey not only personally but professionally. The journey has been filled with ups and downs, with unexpected intellectual revelations and "explosions," and by an awakening to a body of knowledge that has gone well beyond any expectations I could have reasonably imagined. I entered my research journey in 2008 as a confident chief executive officer with over 20 years of global business experience. I quickly realized the extent of the theoretical and intellectual gaps I had. Business schools and businesses in general do not offer comprehensive tools for learning what value and pricing management really is, where it comes from, and what drives managers to act the way they do. In that sense, this book is a compilation of rich and diversified knowledge, philosophical aspirations, and a renewed sense to lead organizations for successful transformations.

This book is the result of many interviews, discussions, meetings, and constructive arguments with hundreds of pricing practitioners. I thank all of them for their continued support and for challenging my thinking about what it takes to be successful in pricing. In fact, I dedicate all this work to the pricing profession and to the thousands of pricing professionals trying to make a difference in their organizations while sometimes facing strong headwinds!

It has been my great fortune and a great privilege to have been guided on this transformational research and philosophical journey by an incredibly dedicated, committed, and caring group of individuals. I am indebted to them not only for leading me through the transformation but also for guiding me on how to þlock biases, fight mental locks, and soften inflexible practitioners' views in a way that led to the delivery of this excellent and unbiased body of work. I only hope that they can be confident of my appreciation and gratitude, as well as the high regard in which I hold all of them. I thank Dick Boland, who gave me the necessary inspiration and skills to create stories, a web of theoretical concepts, and much grounding as a social and philosophical researcher. Andreas Hinterhuber provided strong support for this book as a practitioner scholar. His knowledge in pricing and value management is second to none. The depth and breadth of his intellect provided continuous challenge to my daily work and constant stimulation to get my work published in academic and practitioners' circles. Gary Hunter has been a constant source of inspiration and was kind enough to share guidance on how to get my work to audiences, how to refine my theoretical propositions, and how to relate pricing to the world of account management. Finally, Toni Somers was always responsive and accessible. She was also instrumental in teaching me how to apply the science of statistics to my work. I thank her for her kindness and patience along the way.

Research cannot be accomplished without access to respondents and without good data collection. For this, I will be forever grateful to the Professional Pricing Society and their staff, as well as to the Strategic Account Management Association and their staff. Both organizations graciously gave me access to their membership bases. They also allowed me to present findings to selected groups of members and gave me excellent feedback along the way.

Finally, I am most grateful to my creative and writing team for their steadfast support, patience, and positive energy over the duration of the writing exercise. Bennett Voyles challenged my writing style, provided constructive editing, and guided me in the art of storytelling. Alexis Antes put the final formatting touches to the manuscript to make it what it is today. They have been my strongest advocates in the face of many writing challenges, which have truly humbled me. This book simply could not have been completed without their responsiveness, can-do attitude, and positive energy!

The Pricing Journey

Introduction

Business scholars agree that nothing can add profit to a company's bottom line as quickly as a successful price increase: a 1 percent price increase at an S&P 1500 company typically yields an 8 percent increase in profit (Marn, Roegner, and Zawada 2004). We now know a lot about pricing. And value-based pricing can be pursued without changing one's product, marketing, or company structure—although a pricing shift may, in the end, drive changes to all three. Yet people talk much more about changes in pricing than they actually make them. Why is that?

The reason that shifts in pricing are not more popular is not a matter of technical difficulty—although this can come into play. Nor is it that these changes are great only in theory; hundreds of companies have made them successfully. In fact, companies are mostly held back by myths. Many managers believe, for instance, that pricing can work only if you're a leader in your industry. Not true. They also believe that you must be prepared to make a major investment—also untrue. They have heard that it's practically impossible and tell horror stories about companies that tried and failed to adopt advanced pricing practices. What professionals don't understand is that the failures don't occur because of pricing; they occur primarily because managers fundamentally misunderstand the pricing challenge. As with so many challenges in business, companies have a healthy respect for the technical difficulty of a pricing transformation but are often unprepared to tackle the emotional and behavioral demands of such a change.

I learned this lesson the hard way when I led my first pricing revolution.

In 1998, I was a market manager for the Latin American division of Owens Corning, the building materials and fiberglass company. I was based in Boca Raton, Florida, but one day our headquarters in Toledo called: they needed someone in Belgium to deploy an enterprise resource planning solution across continental Europe, and they chose me. I was perfect for the job: I'm French, I'm a bit aggressive, and maybe best of all, I was still young and naïve enough to accept what a more experienced manager would have recognized at once as a suicide mission.

My Mission Impossible required deploying an advanced and customized pricing module to integrate the hodgepodge of discounts and rebates Owens Corning offered across Europe at the time. Each country and practically each plant had its own pricing schedule. I embarked on a long pricing simplification exercise, which included analyzing the current process in place and developing simplified blueprints. As I progressed in the analysis, supported by a terrific team of IT and business experts, I realized that the company's pricing structure was a mess—fragmented by country and irrationally managed. Our margins were all over the place. As a first step, the team drew up a blueprint with a centralized pricing structure, including standardized rebates and discounts.

The new structure drew a strong reaction, but not the kind I'd hoped for. Salespeople called me up to yell at me. People screamed at me in public. Someone even threw papers at me during a meeting. Who was I? What did I think I was doing? How did I expect them to close deals without any flexibility? Despite excellent preparation and a proactive communication plan, I still became the sales guys' public enemy number one. The deployment ended, and it was considered a success—but I'd crossed enough colleagues that I soon had to move on to a new company.

After it was all over, I reflected about what I'd just gone through. Why were people so upset when most experts agreed that more rational pricing would help the company in the end? Certainly, getting between a sales rep and his or her commission is always dangerous, but this resistance felt like more than that. And why was the company's pricing process such a mess to begin with, anyway? Why hadn't they set things up in a smarter way? After all, these were smart guys—Owens Corning invented fiberglass technology! Even stranger, the more I looked into it, the more I learned that Owens Corning was not unusual. Many companies had similar issues with their pricing. Not only were prices far from optimized, they often weren't formally organized. Managers set prices without much strategic thought, usually according to some combination of mechanical accounting, gut instinct, and the hunger of the sales reps. Money was not only being left on the table—it was being scattered all over the kitchen.

Looked at from one angle, my experience was a professional disaster. But from another, it led me to find an enormous opportunity. At a time when most aspects of business operations were being optimized to three decimal points, pricing was a new frontier that few companies had crossed. Relatively few companies had thought strategically about pricing, although most research suggested that a smarter pricing structure could add 2 to 4 percent more to a company's bottom line, without any other changes (2012). And nobody seemed to have realized what I'd learned in all those angry meetings: the technical challenge was not the biggest challenge in pricing. The biggest challenge was behavioral and emotional.

Fifteen years later, I know a lot more about what a pricing journey is and should look like. I've led several more pricing transformations and conducted a variety of research studies about the emotional and human side of strategic pricing—enough to fill two books before this one. I have learned a lot about pricing. I have discovered that both the art and science of pricing are rich in concepts, methods, approaches, and theories but held back by almost as many myths. I interviewed many experts and professionals in pricing and discovered that the profession has come a long way over the last few decades.

The Evolution of Pricing

Part of the reason this book hasn't been written until now is that the discipline is still so young.

Until the late 1980s, pricing decisions were often made by gut instinct alone, typically by "an outcast in the Marketing or Accounting department with limited upward mobility or gravitas within their company" (Mitchell 2012:404). This person was largely self-taught, and his or her work tended to be "at the mercy of a cross-functional menagerie that likely had very different goals and ideas" (Mitchell 2012:405). Dreams of growing market share or sales volume tended to outweigh margin goals, and particularly for businesses that involved large-ticket items, management was reluctant to embark on any strategy that might cost a sale. For the rank and file too, bonuses were often set on volume triggers, not profitability—and employees usually did what they were encouraged to do.

By the early 1990s, however, a small but steadily growing band of executives and academics began to realize that more careful attention to the pricing lever could yield greater profits. A few textbooks were published that focused exclusively on pricing, and in 1991, Eric Mitchell launched the first professional pricing journal. Conferences and seminars followed. Better pricing software became available. Despite sales reps' grousing that pricing managers' ability to block unprofitable deals had turned the pricing department into the sales prevention department, pricing managers gained stature in some of the world's most sophisticated companies.

Only well into the first decade of the new millennium, however, did most large corporations begin to think systematically about how to raise their pricing power and develop new value propositions to enhance profitability. A lot of them expanded their pricing departments, and some even created vice president–level positions. Several top business schools, including Wharton, Stanford, and the University of Chicago, decided to make pricing education an important part of their executive education programs. The University of Rochester and a few other companies developed a concentration in pricing. Wall Street began considering pricing strength as an important valuation metric, and in 2011, pricing strategists received an important vindication when billionaire investor Warren Buffett said he prized pricing power even above management acumen when it came to making a valuation. Today, pricing is now a regularly explored topic among top-rated practitioners and in academic journals, including the *Journal of Marketing, Harvard Business Review, MIT Sloan Management Review,* and *McKinsey Quarterly,* and pricing scholars have their own journal, the *Journal of Revenue and Pricing Management.* These publications not only propose the latest advances in pricing science but share the results of evidence-based research projects aimed at advancing managerial pricing practices.

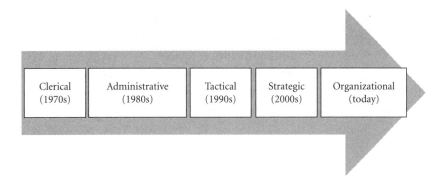

Figure I.1 Evolution of the pricing discipline over the years

Clearly, pricing sophistication had come a long way over the past 20 years, as shown in Figure I.1. Although pricing is no longer seen as a strictly clerical and administrative chore, it still hasn't quite made the evolutionary leap to the status of a strategic function on the order of procurement or supply chain management. Today, awareness of pricing power continues to build—but slowly as ever. This is frustrating for pricing professionals like me who have experienced firsthand the promise of pricing on the bottom line. The art and science of pricing is rich in concepts, methods, tools, scientific approaches, and schools of thought ready for the taking. We have more believers every day, but the divide is still so broad, it's almost ludicrous. We're flying jet engines, but many people in the business world are still saying, "Jeez, Wilbur, what makes you think that contraption is going to fly?"

Pricing Is a Powerful Discipline

The slow adoption of pricing is surprising, given that studies continue to demonstrate that successful price increases have an outsized impact on profit: a +5 percent increase in price may raise earnings before interests and taxes (EBIT) 22 percent, nearly double the impact of a +5 percent increase on revenues (12 percent) (Hinterhuber 2008b). A price hike also tends to be eleven times as effective as a 5 percent rise in R&D investment, which tends to yield just 2 percent more revenue (Hinterhuber 2004). Other studies have also confirmed that smarter pricing is just the smart thing to do:

- Pricing optimization software improves total revenue by 2 to 4 percent, paying back its investment in two years, according to a Gartner study published in 2012.

- Operating margins increase by an average of 3.2 percent 18 to 24 months after implementation of a pricing optimization program, mostly through better price execution and better price setting, according to Deloitte Research.

- Firms that invest in a pricing transformation typically achieve a 3 percent increase in total revenues within two years, according to The Pricing Cloud, a consulting boutique.

- Firms that deployed value-based pricing can expect an increase in gross and profit margins of between 3 and 6 percent, according to a 2013 survey we conducted with 144 pricing professionals with the support of LeveragePoint Innovation, a value-based pricing software firm.

In fact, a 2012 study by Simon-Kucher & Partners, a German consultancy known for its pricing expertise, found that companies with a dedicated pricing function tend to enjoy more pricing power, a greater likelihood of having had a successful price increase last year, and increased margins after that increase. Not coincidentally, they found that the biggest investors in pricing expertise include the world's largest and most sophisticated firms. For the rest, this kind of pricing capability remains unknown. Price setters in smaller organizations continue to believe in myths that were exposed in academic articles years ago.

The call—almost a plea—by consultants and scholars to use and implement value-based pricing strategies is now practically unanimous. However, managers stick with cost-based strategies that sell their company short because they don't consider what the customer is willing to pay (Liozu and Hinterhuber 2013). Overall, only 17 percent of companies use value-based pricing (Hinterhuber 2008b), 40 percent of firms set their prices just by following what their competitors do (Liozu and Hinterhuber 2012b), and the rest set prices using a formula-based approach. The CEOs I interviewed in 2012 told me they believe that strategic pricing can improve profitability and swear that their employees are actively engaged in pricing projects. Most say they understand what other companies have been able to achieve through better pricing, but I have reason to believe the lessons have not really sunk in: when asked about their personal time allocation, only 16 percent devoted any time at all to price management—a clear indication that pricing is not yet treated as a true strategic lever. Nor are they putting their money where their mouth is. In 2012, Zilliant reported that companies spend almost 94 percent less on information technology to help them optimize what they are paid compared to what they pay: $200 million on price-setting software compared to $3 billion on software that optimizes their procurement strategies.

So why the disconnect between theory and practice? My theory is that pricing experts have not thought enough about the social and behavioral aspects of price setting. Marketing scholars and behavioral economists have developed all kinds of theories about pricing behavior in competitive markets and have investigated pricing from the consumer's point of view, but few have considered the emotional side of pricing practices from the perspective of the price setter. Practitioners, meanwhile, have focused only on the technical and scientific dimensions of pricing. They deploy advanced methods and technical tools without adopting a user perspective and without considering the change-management dimension. But I know from experience, confirmed by research, that developing a pricing program isn't just a matter of setting prices and making scientific decisions. It's about making those prices stick, getting users to use advanced pricing tools in their day-to-day activities, and making everyone in the organization believe in them. Finally, more often than not, value-based pricing demands deep and surprisingly painful organizational changes (structure, mind-sets, incentives, reporting lines, etc.).

Toward a New Understanding of Pricing

Setting up a pricing process is hard. It's hard technically, because it's complicated. It's also hard because it demands that people change habits and behaviors that evolved over decades. You can't just flip a switch. Instead, the habits required to maintain a pricing shift must be gradually internalized and embedded in the fabric of the firm. A pricing transformation is the organizational equivalent of genetic engineering. You can bolt on all the software you like, and hire as many analysts as the budget will bear, but a price management program won't achieve anything lasting unless it is slowly and carefully integrated into your firm's DNA. Changing deeply ingrained behaviors takes time.

The purpose of this book is to help executives succeed with the change management that pricing almost always entails. We review the organizational and behavioral factors a company needs to achieve pricing excellence, offer some practical tips and tools to help you as a pricing ambassador, lead your company through each of the five stages of this transformational process, and give you a strong theoretical foundation to help you make the case that the emotional and financial investment required will be worth it.

This book is based on what I learned conducting a series of surveys and interviews with hundreds of executives in collaboration with Andreas Hinterhuber; my own experiences in leading a pricing transformation during my five years as CEO of ARDEX Americas, one of North America's largest manufacturers of specialty cements and building products; and dozens of pricing engagements with a variety of companies in my own consulting practice.

You will find references to many others' research here as well, principally the work of scholars who helped me understand the importance that change management must play in any pricing transformation. In some chapters, you will find a section called "what literature is telling us," designed to inform you about the theoretical sources of some of the concepts we have used in our research journey. This background may make *The Pricing Journey* a little denser than the typical business book, but as they used to say in the old American Express commercials, don't leave home without it. Certainly, you can follow my recommendations for managing a pricing transformation without that theoretical background, but in my view, a deep understanding of its dynamics will help you navigate your own pricing transformation, give you a greater conviction of the importance of sticking to your transformational program, and make it easier to convince your colleagues that pricing is an essential part of your strategy going forward.

In addition, I wanted to give you the full benefit of my own experience, and my research was an important part of that. For me, not sharing this information with you would have been irresponsible, like being a doctor who just gave you a prescription without explaining what the pills were for and what their side effects may be. This may take a little longer, but I'll keep it as simple as I can, and I think you'll be more likely to follow the advice once you understand the reasons behind it.

The Research Foundation

This book is the product not just of my practical experiences but of deep reading into the literature of pricing and change management and a number of large-scale surveys of pricing practitioners. My overall research agenda was informed by my understanding of common problems of pricing practice, my strong practitioner experience, and leading theories on change management. The general lack of attention to and interest in the field of pricing, particularly organizational dimensions of the pricing journey, served as a kind of vacuum that shaped my work.

My research started with the definition of the current trends in pricing literature and by the frequency of project failures with pricing transformations. I needed to develop a comprehensive and contextual description of the concept of both pricing and organizational capabilities. I wanted to apply a mix of theoretical and methodological approaches to the research to develop the holistic understanding I needed. The integration of these multiple research studies happened during the interpretation phase, where I used data results to derive integrated findings and to construct a holistic understanding of what it takes to manage a company through a pricing transformation. This research approach allowed me to use both inductive and deductive reasoning to generate a novel theory of pricing capabilities and to validate my theory through survey research (Van de Ven 2007).

With Andreas Hinterhuber, I conducted the following academic studies over a four-year period:

1. Qualitative interviews with 44 managers in 15 firms in 10 U.S. states (2010)

2. Quantitative study of 748 pricing practitioners on the 5C model (2011)

3. Quantitative study of 557 CEOs and business owners (2011)

4. Quantitative study of 507 commercial managers on pricing confidence (2011)

5. Qualitative study with 16 top pricing leaders in the world on confidence (2011)

6. Quantitative study of 939 pricing practitioners on organizational change capacity (2012)

We used the results of these studies to develop our 5C model of pricing transformation and to identify the activities that managers can design and implement to advance from step to step of the transformational model. I have also tested these steps in consulting engagement in Europe and the United States, and the model has been validated by a number of practitioners around the world. I hope they will resonate with you as well, and that you will be able to apply insights that will make your own pricing journey better and more productive.

Armed with the knowledge of what pricing is all about, how it has evolved over the past decades, and an amazing amount of new data, I propose a new thesis about what pricing excellence means and how you can reach it, or at least aim for it. I start with important definitions, propose a transformational model, and help you with some of the roadblocks you might encounter along the way. I want to give you the keys to better pricing!

The Keys to Better Pricing

I often remind pricing practitioners of the richness of today's pricing discipline. And I also remind them that pricing may mean different things for different people. Definitions matter! Throughout this book, whenever I use the term *pricing*, I am not talking about a mechanical exercise, but the sophisticated, modern, and progressive discipline that includes value-based pricing, strategic pricing, and advanced pricing science.

The key to achieving more control in pricing is to view pricing as a disruptive technical innovation. As with the adoption of any other powerful new tool, the organization needs to master the mechanics and overcome the discomfort of a new way of doing business. In the next ten chapters, I will show you how to do it.

Pricing excellence can be achieved only by taking a strategic view of one's pricing orientation and pricing realization. A company needs both to achieve pricing power over time. Chapter 1 introduces you to the building blocks of pricing excellence and prepares you for the journey ahead. The road ahead entails a five-stage transformation. Chapter 2 provides an overview of these phases. None of these stages is easy, and every company's journey will be slightly different, depending on its industry and culture. However, every company's journey requires 5 Cs: capabilities, champions, change capacity, center-led design, and confidence. Each of these factors plays a critical role in improving the company's pricing power, and each is the subject of a chapter that follows.

Successful pricing journeys need champions to break down barriers, remove pockets of resistance, pay close attention to the transformational pace, and constantly communicate a vision to keep everyone focused on the need for change. The role of these champions is the subject of Chapter 3. Generally, champions must be high enough in the hierarchy to have the credibility and charisma to charm the organization into action; they also must have enough clout to enforce behavior. But the champion's work is not just cheerleading. Typically, he or she must be directly involved, investing significant time, for instance, in the day-to-day aspects of the pricing shift.

One important way to make pricing more strategic and relevant in an organization is to increase the focus with which pricing decisions are made. And for this, the champions of pricing in the C-suite play an important role. Chapter 4 introduces center-led pricing management—a hybrid organizational architecture that combines the advantages of a centralized and a decentralized structure. The centralization of pricing expertise and knowledge allows pricing and business professionals in decentralized structures to make wiser pricing decisions, implement more technical pricing resources, and better manage their tactical pricing operations. In this hybrid model, compliance is gained through communication, coordination, conversation, and consensus. Firms that adopt center-led teams often call them pricing excellence teams, marketing excellence teams, or simply internal consulting teams. The roles and activities of these specialized experts can strongly and positively impact the adoption of the organizational change agenda if pricing champions have designed and communicated a corporate pricing vision.

Pricing capabilities include the skills, technical resources, and activities every company needs to manage its prices. Chapter 5 looks at the skills and resources that companies need to achieve pricing excellence, showing both the relationship between pricing capabilities and firm performance and the organizational capabilities needed to sustain the transformational journey.

The organization's capacity to change is a critical aspect of a pricing transformation. Pricing professionals of the future will be required to serve as change agents as the role of technology in pricing continues to grow. They will need to be able to convince decision makers all over the firm (including sales, marketing, and finance) that a new system needs to be adopted. Through role-playing, coaching sessions, and group exercises, this capability can be strengthened. Chapter 6 will show readers how.

Perhaps the most powerful force needed to drive a pricing transformation is confidence. The team needs to believe in the new pricing structure— to "drink the Kool-Aid." Respondents who took our surveys and who use advanced pricing practices try to appeal to employees on a deeply emotional level in their training initiatives to drive their strategy home and boost confidence levels. In Chapter 7, I propose 24 specific programs to boost collective confidence and help build a team of "pricing superheroes" who are able to overcome price objections in a single bound, selling the company's offerings in a way that sounds neither arrogant nor defensive.

The journey toward pricing excellence typically takes from four to seven years, which means that pricing professionals and executive sponsors need to be ready for plenty of roadblocks—the topic of Chapter 8. All kinds of problems can stall a pricing initiative along the way: lack of will and support from top executives, lack of balanced focus between technical and social dimensions of change, lack of patience and the wish for short-term gains, and potential breakdowns due to market turbulence can all weaken the organization's drive and shake the courage of would-be champions. Finally, the lack of proper map can bring a transformation to a halt. In this chapter, I will provide some recommendations on how to deal with these potential roadblocks so that your pricing journey can stay on the right track.

Pricing has come a long way in the past ten years, thanks to the emergence of pricing software, better pricing strategies, and many excellent pricing books. But many myths are surprisingly resilient, particularly when it comes to the costs and benefits of undergoing a pricing transformation. All kinds of fallacies regarding time allocation constraints, firm size, and payback expectations continue to persist. When you act as a pricing change agent, knowing how to respond to them will save you time. Chapter 9 will provide insights on how to respond to these myths and how to make sure your organization understands the truth about pricing and its potential to improve profitability and raise the caliber of an organization.

Pricing practitioners may not realize it yet, but as in so many fields, technology will soon perform most of the analytical and predictive activities of pricing. As a result, the role of the pricing professional will continue to evolve, and the nature of the work will change. As machines and software potentially handle more and more of pricing's technical aspects, pricing practitioners will focus more on its emotional and organizational side—the spots the computers can't reach, which are the focus of Chapters 3 through 7. I believe that in the future, training programs will reflect this new dynamic. Pricing practitioners will need to drive challenging pricing programs that incorporate an ever-increasing level of business complexity. In fact, managing complexity in pricing and value will become a must-have in most future pricing executive job descriptions. Chapter 10 takes us into the future briefly to explore these skills and explain how the contents of this book can serve as the basis of your continued success in pricing as the field evolves.

In Chapter 11, I propose five concluding considerations that are critical for practitioners who are ready and willing to get started. Finally, I integrate the 5C model in a short case study about my experience at ARDEX Americas.

After reading these eleven chapters, you will have a clearer idea of what a pricing transformation will demand of your company, its complex challenges, and its considerable rewards. I hope too that you will be able to see the potential of pricing not simply as a way to raise your margins, but as a tool to revitalize your company. In the end, pricing excellence demands not only that you understand your organization, but that you understand your customer. Price discovery is ultimately a journey of self-discovery. If your company is like most companies, the executives probably talk a lot about wanting to be more customer-centered, but you won't achieve it until you understand at a profound level why, how, and how deeply the customer values your offering.

Now let's get started.

1 What Is Pricing Excellence?

Renowned investor Warren Buffett once said, "The single most important decision in evaluating a business is pricing power. If you've got the power to raise prices without losing business to a competitor, you've got a very good business. And if you have to have a prayer session before raising the price by 10%, then you've got a terrible business" (Frye and Campbell 2011).

Although the Oracle of Omaha is far from alone in seeing pricing strength as closely linked to the health of a business, the actual practice of pricing receives scant attention in most companies. McKinsey & Company estimates that fewer than 15 percent of companies conduct any systematic research before they set their prices (Mitchell 2011). One reason for the lack of interest may be that nearly two thirds of companies lack pricing power. In their 2011 study of global pricing practices, Simon-Kucher & Partners found that 65 percent of companies had low pricing power and only 35 percent had high pricing power, which Simon-Kucher defines as the ability of a company to get all or nearly all "the money it deserves for the value it delivers."

Most companies with low pricing power blame a cutthroat environment of competitive pricing (71 percent) and customers with strong buying power (36 percent). But at least one statistic suggests that many companies are overly pessimistic: Simon-Kucher found that nearly half (46 percent) of those surveyed believe their company is fighting a price war, and most of the besieged (83 percent) blame their competitors for starting it—a combination that doesn't quite make sense: how could a price war always be the other company's fault? By contrast, companies with high pricing power tend to believe they deserve it, thanks to a stronger brand (75 percent) and a premium product (49 percent), according to Simon-Kucher's survey (2012).

End of story? Not quite. In fact, neither the winners nor the losers are right about how they got to where they are. As you will learn in the next section, pricing power does not automatically correlate with value. Instead, pricing power correlates much more closely with pricing skills. My research suggests that price setting and price getting require discipline, not luck. A survey of 748 members of the Professional Pricing Society, conducted in April 2011, found that although external factors such as competitive intensity affect pricing power, companies have much more control than they think they do over the prices they charge. Even controlling for firm size, nature, main activity, and function of respondents, pricing capabilities had a positive and significant correlation with firm performance (pricing performance, sales performance, and financial performance). The evidence suggests that almost any business can improve its pricing performance, provided it approaches pricing in a structured way.

More specifically, the survey found the following:

- The behavior of an internal champion for pricing had a positive and significant impact on relative firm performance, pricing capabilities, and organizational confidence for pricing.
- Center-led pricing management had a significant impact on the design and development of pricing capabilities.
- The capacity of an organization to change its prices relates positively and significantly to the level of pricing capabilities, to the level of organizational confidence in pricing, and to relative firm performance.
- Pricing capabilities had a positive and significant influence on organizational confidence in pricing.
- And this confidence is a good thing: as with pricing capabilities, organizational confidence itself has a positive and significant influence on relative firm performance.

Most significantly, the analysis showed that pricing capabilities are the most important survey factor in a firm's relative overall pricing performance—accounting for over *34 percent of the variance*—more than any other factor, including organizational confidence (22 percent), change capacity (11 percent), and championing behaviors (10 percent). Several other studies have likewise confirmed that pricing has a substantial impact on company profitability. Simon-Kucher & Partners estimates that two thirds of all companies give up as much as 25 percent of their profits through weak pricing practices (2011). Even small variations in price can raise or lower profitability by as much as 20 to 50 percent (Hinterhuber 2004).

But firms that decide they would like to achieve pricing excellence face two problems. First, no one can quite agree about how to define pricing excellence; ask 100 pricing practitioners what pricing excellence means and you'll get 100 different answers. Second, nobody can fully agree on a road map or process on how to achieve it. You can learn a lot from the great pricing thinkers—Tom Nagle, John Hogan, Ken Monroe, Hermann Simon, Gerald Smith, and Robert Dolan, just to mention a few—but no one in the profession, not even the profession itself, has really developed a standard road map that shows how you make the long journey from pricing weakness to pricing strength. Until now.

The Pricing Capability Grid

The Pricing Capability Grid changes that. It defines pricing excellence and suggests the best paths you can take to get there. It frames the concept of pricing excellence into a grid on two axes: pricing orientation and pricing realization.

The grid is the outcome of our own experience as pricing practitioners and extensive research. In 2011, I interviewed 44 executives to learn more about the nature of pricing capabilities. Their companies varied in size from about 50 to more than 2,000 employees and differed dramatically in their pricing capabilities. I spoke to CEOs and CFOs, heads of business units and professionals in marketing, and heads of pricing and finance functions in fifteen U.S.-based industrial companies about their pricing practices and capabilities, and tried to find out why pricing skills tended to be so undervalued (Liozu et al. 2011).

To capture contrasting perspectives on pricing within companies, I narrowed my search down to businesses with at least three respondents, each at a different management level, including at least one respondent from top management (either a CEO, a managing director, or a member of the board of management), one respondent from middle management (either a business unit manager or a head of a functional unit), and one respondent from lower management (a functional manager). Of the 36 companies meeting these criteria, 15 agreed to participate in this research project. At least three interviews were conducted at each company. Respondents included 15 CEOs or top executives, 18 sales and marketing managers with full or partial responsibility for pricing, and 11 finance and accounting managers with decision-making authority.

In the course of this research, I concluded that pricing power is not a destiny that depends on your market position, but a learned behavior. While competition, costs, and price sensitivity within a market affect the parameters within which companies set prices, superior pricing is almost always based on skills. The companies in my survey that had achieved better pricing all had high-level managers who championed the development of skills in price setting (price orientation) and price getting (price realization). Regardless of their industry, the degree to which managers focused on developing these two capabilities correlated with their success in getting a better price for their product than their competitors (Liozu and Hinterhuber 2012b). Without managerial engagement, companies typically fall back on historical heuristics, such as cost information, to set prices, and yield too much pricing authority to the sales force.

To rank the relative development of the company's pricing function, we created and operationalized the Pricing Capability Grid (Figure 1.1). We categorized pricing abilities into five major categories: the Pricing Power Zone, the Value Surrender Zone, the Price Capture Zone, the Zone of Good Intentions, and the White Flag Zone. Companies in the Pricing Power Zone command significantly higher prices and profitability levels than companies in the White Flag Zone. Most of these companies had undergone a long and difficult transformation that enabled them to evolve from traditional, cost-based pricing toward higher-margin pricing with more disciplined pricing execution. But when they finished, they had achieved something impossible according to traditional pricing theory: they had essentially learned their way to better prices.

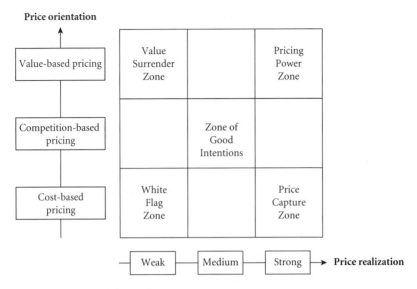

Figure 1.1 Pricing Capability Grid

Pricing capabilities have two dimensions: price setting and price getting, and all companies fit into one of five squares it creates.

Price Setting

Price setting (price orientation) is how a company determines its final selling prices. Companies differ wildly in their approach to price setting. However, although companies that sell services to individual consumers, for example, may price differently than companies that sell jet engines to sophisticated purchasing centers, and pricing approaches in India may differ considerably from pricing approaches in France, my own experience—and most academic research supports this—suggests that pricing methods across industries, countries, and companies usually fall into one of three buckets: cost-based pricing, competition-based pricing, or customer value-based pricing (Liozu and Hinterhuber 2013; Hinterhuber 2008b).

- *Cost-based pricing* decisions are influenced primarily by accounting data, with the objective of reaching a certain return on investment or markup on costs. Typical examples of cost-based pricing approaches are cost-plus pricing, target return pricing, markup pricing, and break-even pricing. The main advantage of this approach is for the price setter: the data you need to set the prices are usually easy to find. The main weakness of cost-based pricing is that aspects related to demand (willingness to pay, price elasticity) and competition (competitive price levels) are ignored.

- *Competition-based pricing* uses data on competitive price levels or on anticipated or observed actions of actual or potential competitors as a primary source to determine appropriate price levels. The main advantage of this approach is that it incorporates a view of the competition. The main disadvantage is that it again ignores demand. In addition, an aggressive response to a competitor's price can raise the risk of a price war, which at extremes may not only hurt the profitability of one company but destroy the profitability of an entire industry. The kinds of scorched-earth wars that hit the U.S. domestic car market between 2005 and 2009 and the U.S. airline industry around the same time are good examples of the damage an all-out price war can inflict. Competition-based pricing approaches are frequently justified on the grounds that price is one of the customer's most important purchase criteria, but if it triggers a war that leads to widespread bankruptcies, it's hard to see how those unsustainable bargains benefit the consumer in the long run.

- *Customer value-based pricing*, often called "value-based pricing," uses analytics about the customer's perceived value of the product or service as the main factor for determining the final selling price. Instead of asking, "How can we realize higher prices despite intense competition?" customer value-based pricing asks, "How can we create additional customer value and increase customer willingness to pay, despite intense competition?" The subjective value of a purchase offering to actual and potential customers is the primary driver in setting prices. Customer value-based pricing approaches require a deep understanding of customer needs, customer perceptions of value, price elasticity, and customers' willingness to pay. Or as one executive explained to me:

> Value-based pricing I think is, in my mind, simple. It's what the customer is prepared to pay based on what the product does for the customer, and that they perceive it will do for them.

The advantage of customer value-driven pricing approaches is their direct link to the customer. Their big disadvantage is that data on customer preferences, willingness to pay, price elasticity, and size of different market segments are usually hard to find and interpret. Customer value-based pricing approaches may also lead to relatively high prices, especially for unique products. That may sound good, but if your prices are too high you can encourage new entrants to join the market or create a huge opportunity for competitors to sell comparable products at slightly lower prices. Finally, customers must first recognize value before they are willing to pay for it, which can be a problem if you have just introduced a genuinely superior product. Often, marketers must educate prospective customers to recognize the product's superiority before linking price to value.

Despite these shortcomings, many pricing scholars consider customer value-based pricing to be the best way to set new-product prices or to adjust prices for existing products (Anderson and Narus 1998; Anderson, Wouters, and van Rossum 2010). Some businesspeople have also found that customer value-based pricing can have important benefits, especially in highly competitive industries (Ingenbleek et al. 2003). This may seem counterintuitive, but it's not. Many managers mistakenly assume they are stuck in a "commodity" business. They overlook possibilities for differentiation and customer value creation and resign themselves to competing solely on price. While some segments in an industry may become severely price competitive, most of us give up the fight too easily. In fact, thinking of your product as a commodity is a good way to make it a commodity. Through deeper research into customer needs, almost any product or service can be differentiated. Such research can also be a powerful weapon to overcome price pressure by retailers. Armed with data on customer willingness to pay, price elasticities, and perceptions of value and price, manufacturers can demonstrate to retailers the total value jointly created through their value-based pricing strategy.

Price Getting

Companies also differ in their abilities to realize the prices they set. Price getting (or more formally, price realization) refers to the capabilities and processes that ensure that the price the company gets is as close as possible to the price the company sets. Why would those two numbers differ? One reason is inconsistent discount systems (Sodhi and Sodhi 2005). The abilities of sales reps to negotiate and levels of authority among sales managers vary widely, enabling some customers to obtain much more favorable conditions than others. Also, in order to reach their sales quota, IT-savvy sales associates sometimes override the discount control systems, even as colleagues try to protect prices and margins, preferring to walk away from deals below well-defined target prices. Price-getting capabilities are thus fundamentally related to a company's ability to translate goals into results; they reflect the capacity and will of a company to enforce—both internally through sales personnel and externally through customers and trade partners—its list prices and to translate these list prices into the prices the company actually gets (Nagle and Holden 2002; Dutta et al. 2002).

Our research indicates that differences in price-getting capabilities reflect a slew of factors:

- The existence of pricing rules specifying maximum discount levels for any given order size
- The extent to which these rules and guidelines are followed
- The individual and organizational consequences for not following these guidelines
- The extent to which sales personnel have to justify and ask for approval for deviating from list prices
- The negotiation skills of sales personnel
- The degree to which sales associates understand a customer's best available alternative
- The customer's maximum willingness to pay and the differential value to customers of the company's product and service offering
- The existence of clear target prices before sales personnel enter into negotiations with customers
- The amount of pressure (self-imposed or organizational) that pushes sales personnel to conclude unprofitable deals
- The confidence to walk away from unprofitable deals
- The extent of free services offered to customers to close a deal

- The systems in place to monitor and communicate price deviations to sales personnel, marketing managers, and other decision makers

The Five Zones of Pricing

How do the companies in my research sample differ in their price-orientation and price-realization capabilities? Following a thorough review of all fifteen companies in my initial sample and supported by many other practical case studies, I found significant contrasts between companies with strong pricing capabilities and high price realization (Pricing Power Zone) and those with weak pricing capabilities and weak price realization (White Flag Zone). I classified each of the fifteen companies I studied according to its price-setting and price-getting capabilities, and I also identified five primary pricing zones as shown in Figure 1.2. Upon classification of our group of companies in their respective zones, I then named these five zones in order to best represent their current position in the grid.

The Pricing Power Zone (high capabilities in price orientation, high capabilities in price realization). My research identified a limited number of

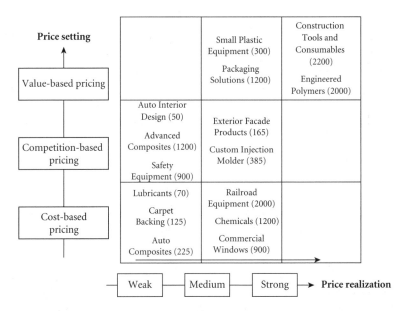

Figure 1.2 Industrial firms in the Pricing Capability Grid

companies with high pricing power. These companies share the following traits: a culture dedicated to pricing, sophisticated tools to quantify customer willingness to pay, customer price elasticities, and robust pricing processes. Perhaps most important of all, they had champions spreading the diffusion of pricing capabilities throughout the organization. These companies typically have high confidence in their ability to implement list price increases and to defend their price levels to buyers. One CEO, managing a mid-sized manufacturing and technology company, described the management challenge this way:

> You only need to be brave for one second, and it's when the guy asks for a discount and you say no. And then you justify it. That takes bravery. So how do you get salespeople in a mindset to justify the price? You don't have to go in there and be Superman for two hours. You have to be Superman for one second.

Beyond assistance in developing those justifications, the superheroes in the front office perform better if they have some super friends backing them up. Companies with superior pricing power tend to have dedicated pricing personnel, such as a chief pricing officer, a head of revenue management, or a director of pricing. These senior executives are responsible for implementing robust organizational processes to ensure that pricing decisions are embedded in robust structures and processes, and not left to the discretion of sales personnel in the field. As one pricing manager at a high-performing building materials company said:

> We have the prices structured in the system . . . the profit desk underneath the pricing team can look to see whether or not the price points are too low, or are at least profitable and value-based enough to go, regardless of what business or trade it is. It's all set up, up front in the system.

Companies with strong pricing capabilities also often have an executive champion driving the price-getting discipline. Executives in most firms are only involved in pricing to approve unusual pricing deviations, to participate in large contract negotiations, or to conduct general business reviews. But executives in companies with strong pricing power all actively engage in improving pricing capabilities and overall system effectiveness. These executives drive the internalization of customer value-based pricing throughout the company and motivate the organizational changes required to support it. The sales and marketing managers we interviewed reported that they found support and conviction from top leaders essential when they adopted customer value-based pricing. As a customer focus manager at a company using customer value-based pricing remarked:

> What made [customer value-based pricing] work was, looking back . . . definitely the fact that top management helped sell it, helped, honestly, push it along as well. And over time, it's proven that they were correct. But without the top management, it wouldn't have happened.

However, value-based pricing isn't for everybody. Companies that already have high pricing power should carefully weigh the costs and benefits of the increased complexity of value-based pricing strategies. As one senior manager at an industrial company put it:

> How many price points do we want to try to manage—how many different price points? Because there is a balance. You can take value and use to every single customer/product combination, and then we've got hundreds of thousands of price points we're trying to manage, which is not good either.

The White Flag Zone (low capabilities in price orientation, low capabilities in price realization). Companies in this sample paid little attention to pricing. Not surprisingly, White Flag companies lagged companies with more pricing power in key profitability indicators. In the White Flag Zone, prices do not reflect the customer's value and willingness to pay, and sales personnel do not have well-crafted guidelines. Whether their list prices are enforced in the field depends mostly on luck and on the salesman's discretion. One CEO of a company using cost-based pricing described the situation this way:

> Pricing is based on the gut of our sales personnel . . . as long as they're within their [pricing] latitude to make decisions.

In these companies, managers complain about declining price levels but lack the capabilities, vision, and instruments to counter these developments. Discounting is widespread and chaotic. In essence, these companies have abdicated their pricing power to their customers.

The Value Surrender Zone (high capabilities in price orientation, weak capabilities in price realization). In companies in or near this zone, list prices generally reflect customer value well. However, such companies also fail to realize the value they have created because discounting guidelines are haphazard. Sales personnel negotiate aggressively with customers to bring deals home but lack the information to truly track and improve price levels. In other words, although these companies excel in value creation and delivery, they leave a lot of money on the table. One sales manager in a company near this zone observed:

> The COO had put in these measures to increase sales by discounting, filling up the plant, and he had convinced the people underneath him . . . that absorption was the name of the game. So now that's embedded in the culture.

The Price Capture Zone (low capabilities in price orientation, high capabilities in price realization). By contrast, companies in this zone have robust systems and processes to make list prices stick. However, they typically use rather unsophisticated methods to set those list prices in the first place. These companies frequently excel in price execution, but their prices do not reflect the full value that their products and services deliver to their customers. As one CEO of a company using cost-based pricing observed:

> The stage gates are you either proceed or don't proceed based on costing—cost targets. We set a cost target based on the margin expectations, then, of the approximate selling price target. So much more of the formality is around, "Are we gonna hit the cost target? Are we way off the cost target?" . . . We put more formality around costing analysis, and there is less formality around the pricing.

Despite simplistic price-setting mechanisms, companies in or near this zone have robust processes to realize target list prices with customers. The challenge for sales in this zone is that success still requires a high level of individual and organizational confidence. One manager in a company near this zone observed:

> You have to look [customers] in the eye and say, "Ours costs more. This costs more, and it's worth it. You should pay more for that." You have to be pretty confident to do that.

The Zone of Good Intentions (average price orientation, average price realization capabilities). The companies stuck in this zone use slightly more advanced approaches for setting prices but haven't reached true pricing sophistication. One company, for example, uses dynamic premium pricing that links its own prices to price levels of a well-defined competitor set. Good Intentions companies also have some systems and processes in place to limit the discretion of sales personnel in the field and to encourage discipline in price realization. However, some barrier, perhaps a strong production orientation, keeps the company focused inward, preventing its pricing capabilities from reaching a high level of maturity. As the CEO of a company using competition-based pricing commented:

> Our DNA is manufacturing . . . I'm very used to standard cost . . . the very traditional cost-plus. It just comes from being a manufacturing company . . . I think we're dynamic and moving in the service models but we've dragged along this cost-plus kind of a pricing model.

The Transformation to Strong Price-Orientation and Price-Realization Capabilities

Virtually all companies aspire to set prices close to the value their products and services deliver and then close the gap between list prices and actual in-pocket prices. Yet few companies have successfully made the transition from cost- or competition-based pricing with weak price-realization capabilities to customer value-based price setting with strong price-realization capabilities. Moving the organization to implement a new pricing approach is a difficult process that significantly exceeds the complexity of activities such as changing list prices (Forbis and Mehta 1981). The managers I interviewed who have implemented value-based pricing all say it requires a deep organizational change that transforms the company's organizational life and identity as well as the identity of actors within it. They said the transformation from pricing based on cost or competition to pricing based on customer value is a difficult process (Liozu, Hinterhuber, Perelli, et al. 2012). It's not just a matter of reprinting the menu; typically, a value-based pricing transformation requires new organizational priorities, a new organizational structure, new capabilities, new processes and tools, and different goal and incentive systems (Liozu et al. 2011). The implementation and internalization of customer value-based pricing capabilities is a long, tedious, and sometimes painful journey of change that can take four to seven years. It requires intense and sustained organizational mobilization to transform established structures, cultures, processes, and systems and demands continual attention, continuous investments, and executive sweat equity (Liozu and Hinterhuber 2012a).

Chances are that when you reach the Pricing Power Zone after several years of hard work, your organization and your pricing process will look completely different (Figure 1.3). Pricing and value management will be ingrained in your organization's DNA. Your marketing and commercial teams will work hand in hand with your pricing professionals. The tools and models used by your teams will be some of the best and most progressive known in the pricing profession. The journey from the White Flag Zone to the Pricing Power Zone is a transformational experience. And that

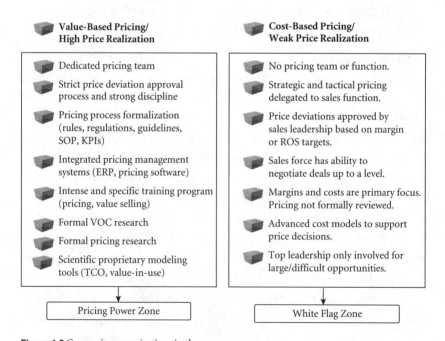

Figure 1.3 Comparing organizations in the zones

transformation will happen at all levels: the way you organize yourself; how you collaborate; how management supports pricing; how advanced tools are adopted and used; and how aligned your teams are.

So you probably know where you're starting. But how do you know where you are going and when you have reached the Pricing Power Zone?

Reaching the Zone

Where should you begin? The Pricing Capability Grid may suggest that investing in better price getting or better price setting would be equally useful. In fact, I find that most of the time, a company is better off shoring up its price-getting capability first: fix your systems, firm up the discipline of your sales force, and establish clearer guidelines regarding pricing policies. Only then should you begin to think about how and when to raise your prices. Companies that try to tackle both challenges at once tend to fail. Another reason to work toward the right of the grid first is that more price-setting changes involve adding new technical capabilities. These tools, skills, and practices can be rolled out incrementally, at a pace that allows your organization to integrate and assimilate this expertise. This takes time, but it will eventually make it possible to move with confidence to the more difficult stage of price setting.

At the beginning, however, the organization will need to make a mental adjustment. Marketers, sellers, and developers have to change their business mentality and frames of reference and embrace new value-related concepts (Forbis and Mehta 1981; Liozu, Hinterhuber, Boland, et al. 2012). They must learn a new language in order to carry the value message internally and externally.

To do all that requires a lot of confidence. When confidence is high, people share a greater belief in their collective power to produce desired outcomes and ends (Bohn 2001); confidence gives the organization a sense of "can do" (Kanter 2006). The question is, where do you get some confidence? Unfortunately, there isn't an app for that, but the good news is that organizational confidence can also be instilled into the organization, just like a skill. In the next chapters, we look at how to boost confidence inside the organization and build an army of "pricing superheroes."

You won't get to the next zone overnight. Most pricing consultants report significant impact to the bottom line only 18 to 24 months after a pricing investment is made. You'll know you've succeeded when the answer to
each of the following questions is yes: Can you launch these products with
the right value messages and the proper value selling programs? Can you
make price changes to the market based primarily on your value proposition and value models and not only on changes in your cost structure? Can
your organization be a true price leader by educating the customer base on
new pricing models, by deploying new pricing strategies, and by being a
consistent leader in making price changes? If you have more nos than yeses,
you still have a ways to go.

No Right Path—But One Right Direction

In the next chapter, I focus on the specific stages a company must pass
through in order to achieve a value-based pricing transformation and
how to design a powerful road map to get through each of those stages.
Although no standard road maps can be used and each organization must
find its own way, I find that moving from left to right on the Pricing Capability Grid seems to work better than the other alternatives (Figure 1.4).

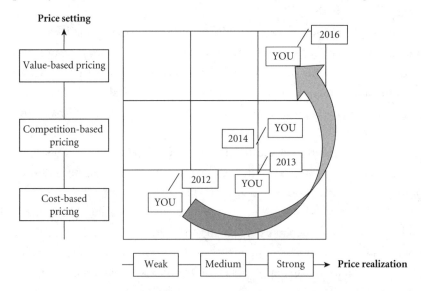

Figure 1.4 The path to pricing excellence

The precise path your company should follow in the Pricing Capability Grid will depend on where you begin. Some organizations may be stuck in the Zone of Good Intentions and then decide to accelerate the transformation of their primary pricing orientation, such as moving up to value-based pricing. Others are already up on the grid and need to reinforce their pricing process and boost their pricing discipline. If your organization is starting from scratch and you are currently in the White Flag Zone, I strongly recommend that you do not make value-based pricing your first priority. By all means discuss your value proposition, your overall differentiation level, and your customer segmentation process, but don't try to implement value-based pricing without having some basic pricing knowledge in place, at least a vague outline of a pricing process, and proper pricing discipline guidelines. Trying to achieve value-based pricing without building such strong internal capabilities first will create confusion and organizational breakdowns. Value is subjective, difficult to identify and measure, and everyone needs to agree on just what it means before you try to launch (Liozu, Hinterhuber, Boland, et al. 2012). Instead, I recommend that you embark on a pricing journey starting from the White Flag Zone or the Zone of Good Intentions and begin working on programs affecting their pricing realization level and their overall pricing discipline as shown in Figure 1.1, including building a pricing organization (pricing team and pricing council), conducting basic and foundational pricing training, and putting a pricing process in place within the business.

In other words, invest first in your pricing process, your pricing function, and your pricing discipline. Only at that point should you try to push your pricing orientation from cost or competition toward customer value. Otherwise, you won't be able to implement value-based pricing, and if you do, it won't work for very long.

Conclusion

Pricing power is often regarded as a predestined condition, the natural reward for having built a better mousetrap. But our research suggests that the truth is more complex and optimistic; although value and pricing discipline matter, most companies with superior pricing power have superior pricing capabilities—and pricing capabilities can be developed. My work focused on small and medium industrial companies, but it can be easily extended to larger companies or business units, judging from the response I've had to my model from hundreds of pricing practitioners during conference presentations, workshops, and consulting engagements. Like the old saying that "You don't get what you deserve, you get what you negotiate," pricing power depends less on value or competitive position than on how well your firm manages the defining moment of any business relationship—the instant the customer reaches for his or her wallet.

2 The Transformational Journey

Despite the fact that everything a company does is aimed toward the moment the customer pays for an offering, companies have traditionally treated pricing as kind of a clerical job. Only recently have marketers and senior executives started thinking about pricing. Yet too often, pricing is still neglected and considered in largely tactical terms.

For the most part, pricing remains a science or discipline that rarely reaches the C-suite (Liozu and Hinterhuber 2011). Most pricing activities and programs are fragmented and disconnected. Pricing innovations emerge at the business-unit level and make slow internal progress until they are eventually adopted across the enterprise. Even many of the largest and most sophisticated companies operate this way. I recently visited a Fortune 500 company in the building-materials sector and met with half a dozen internal pricing professionals, each of whom represented a different business unit. Although they knew each other, they clearly had not spoken much. They had not shared their best practices, let alone developed a strategic vision. With this degree of fragmentation, designing and deploying an enterprise-wide pricing transformation is nearly impossible.

Two words in the title of this chapter sum up the challenge companies face if they want to achieve world-class pricing:

- *Transformational.* Developing a world-class pricing capability requires a transformation: transformational design, transformational leadership, and transformational change.

- *Journey.* A pricing transformation is always a long, hard trip. The dynamic nature of business means you must invest and keep investing and never stop paying attention to pricing management. The good news is that if you can maintain this discipline and continue on a well-planned pricing journey, your pricing capabilities improve. The bad news is that once you start you can never quit. Firms that stop working on their pricing usually start experiencing breakdowns, performance erosion, and organizational dysfunction. The pricing journey never ends.

The Pricing Maturity Model

Over the past few years, I have studied multiple pricing maturity scales (Deloitte, McKinsey, and others). They offer a road map on what to do first, how to do it, and how to deploy various programs, methods, tools, and systems. Their pricing maturity models are especially useful if you are in the market for new technical pricing capabilities.

The most commonly accepted pricing maturity model was designed by Paul Hunt and Jim Saunders. Hunt and Saunders's road map does a good job of describing the technical side of achieving world-class pricing (Hunt and Saunders 2013), as shown in Figure 2.1, and touching on the behavioral and organizational components of the pricing journey. But by and large, these and other models miss a key to succeeding in a pricing journey: the social dimension of technology. The best pricing technology in the world is useless if you can't persuade people to adopt it. A more useful model must incorporate a number of behavioral and organizational factors, including the following:

- A balanced approach between technical pricing capabilities and social capabilities in addition to a heavy focus on tools, methods, software, and analytics
- A practical road map to show pricing practitioners not only what to do but how to move successfully from stage to stage
- A greater focus on human beings at the center of the pricing transformation and on both pricing setters and price users

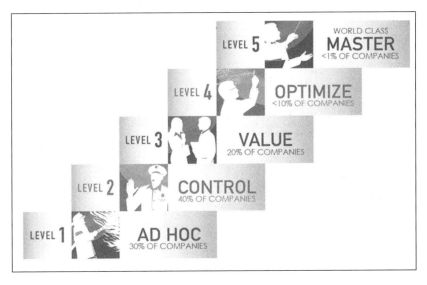

Figure 2.1 Pricing solutions' pricing maturity model

SOURCE: Paul Hunt, Pricing Solutions.

- A recognition that change management is an important dimension of the transformational journey
- Practical tools and steps to increase adoption, assimilation, and usage of pricing tools, methods, and systems
- A greater focus on the uniqueness of each transformational journey, including an understanding that specific pricing capabilities and investments are required that depend on the nature of the company's industry, its organizational culture, and its preexisting political structure
- A multifunctional approach to the pricing journey that helps the pricing function collaborate with other functions around the company, including R&D, innovation, operations, and finance, each of which are critical to the journey toward pricing excellence

These other factors are so complex that traditional models can't really accommodate them. The pricing discipline needs a new multidimensional maturity model that can guide pricing practitioners and business leaders through the multiple levels of technical, cultural, and structural challenges that a pricing transformation entails—and this is what I propose next.

The Transformational Model

As Wharton pricing scholar John Zhang has suggested, not thinking strategically about pricing makes about as much sense as a farmer deciding to take a vacation right around harvest time. However, it is understandable. The exchange of value tends to be emotionally difficult for both buyer and seller—a moment of truth that immediately clarifies the value both parties place on the offering. Price too high and you lose the sale and alienate the potential customer. Price too low and you hurt yourself and maybe compromise the image of your brand. Get it wrong often enough, and you may even go out of business. No wonder, given all the potential for failure, that companies tend to avoid the topic.

Even installing new pricing technology hasn't changed the dynamic. New systems aren't productive when they are invented, but when they are adopted. Only companies that learn to manage both the social and technical aspects of a pricing transformation ever achieve pricing excellence. Nor can a pricing transformation be just partially rolled out; based on my research and practical experience in leading a number of these revolutions, I have found that companies that aspire to pricing excellence pass through five stages of development in their pricing capabilities (Figure 2.2).

Typically, one stage blurs into the next, and in every stage, new technologies and new activities are introduced. Step back, though, and the pricing transformation journey almost always looks like this:

Stage 1. Realization and Exploration

Managers become aware of the nature of their pricing problems and begin to explore potential solutions (Cyert and March 1992; Fiol and O'Connor 2003). Leaders during this phase of introspection—from both top and middle management—recognize that the organization's pricing dynamics are weak. Often, some bad news made them aware of the condition of their pricing structure: discounting irrationality during slower demand cycles, new-product introduction failures, or acquisition of a business with

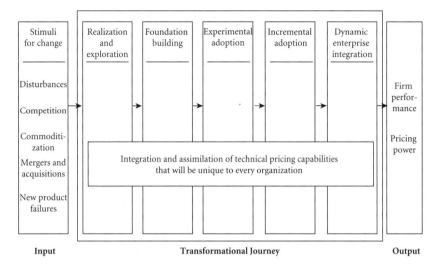

Input	Transformational Journey	Output

Figure 2.2 The transformational model

a more sophisticated pricing orientation (Liozu, Hinterhuber, Perelli, et al. 2012). They begin to search for potential problems and solutions by conducting internal workshops, visiting customers, holding venting sessions, interviewing stakeholders, visiting pricing conferences, discussing the situation with peers, conducting benchmarking, or inviting pricing consulting firms to conduct an initial discovery process. This phase of discovery has the potential to be painful and challenging. *Discovery* is the right term for it. Do not call it a pricing audit! Call it an exploration and discovery phase! As the pricing team starts exploring the root causes of potential pricing problems, with or without the help of consultants, dysfunctional processes and behaviors rise to the surface, creating some potentially tense and explosive organizational dynamics. No one likes to be told that the way they are doing something is wrong, and morale is easily crushed. The best way to conduct this phase of exploration and discovery is through a formal, collaborative, and controlled pricing capabilities assessment (PCA) process. In this process, the content of the PCA can be controlled and communicated as needed. I usually recommend the formation of a multifunctional discovery team that can help identify problems, search for solutions, and, most of all, set priorities. Messages must be carefully crafted to avoid bruising egos. Collaborative discovery and blueprinting of your pricing situation with the right stakeholder has the power to build bonds. Teams search for issues and solutions together, which creates buy-in. A tip here is to bring the sales force early in the discovery process so that they also participate in the brainstorming and solution-searching process. They then have "skin in the game."

Stage 2. Foundation Building

The pricing team begins to develop technical pricing activities, perhaps including training on basic technical concepts. The goal of this stage is to prepare the culture for future pricing programs (Geels 2004). One of its major aims is to give everybody in the organization the same level of pricing knowledge. This requires the design and deployment of many basic training sessions for multiple stakeholders in the organization (sales, innovation, finance, and more). It also involves a continued search for pricing solutions based on the results of a potential pricing capabilities assessment. Successful pricing leaders make sure that as the road map for their pricing journey takes shape, it is based on the particular challenges faced by the organization, the company's current pricing maturity level, and overall level of pricing knowledge. This is where many mistakes are made. Leaders are often in a hurry to deploy advanced pricing resources and assets that the organization is not ready to adopt. The result of such a hurried approach is lack of adoption and potentially a flat-out rejection of the new tools. Other companies may go over this stage very quickly as their organization is mature enough to take on experimental projects and test new pricing solutions.

Leaders must pay close attention to this point to avoid creating a lasting negative impression. At the previously mentioned Fortune 500 company, for example, their early adoption of price optimization software failed because many users would not use it. Pricing experts at the company told me that not only had few people used the software, but its rejection set a precedent for spurning other IT upgrades later on (Lyytinen and Robey 1999). Users remember bad IT deployments; getting a once-burned team to try something new is even more difficult the second time around. At this stage, the focus should be to raise awareness about the potential impact of solving critical pricing issues through a quick win or two. As the pricing foundation is built, generating easy wins or "plugging some holes" can help get people on board to move to Stage 3. Therefore, the goal of this stage of the model is to create transparency and clarity about pricing concepts and priorities so that stakeholders are on the same page with the right amount of preparation. That will boost your initial level of collective confidence.

Stage 3. Experimental Adoption

In the third stage, the team must identify a particular line or unit to test its newly defined pricing models. This is probably the biggest decision of this specific stage. Should you run a pilot project of new pricing models with a struggling business unit or a very successful one? Or should you select a region, a product line, or a whole division? The answer to this question will vary, but in either case, slow but steady adoption tends to work best. A "big bang" project can be dangerous; the risk of failure is too great and a failure can put the whole pricing program in jeopardy. A better choice tends to be a business unit with mild pricing problems and an acceptable level of differentiation and pricing power. Select a manager who understands pricing and has favorable perceptions about it; her chances of success will be greater if she champions the pilot project and fully embraces the pricing road map for her scope of business. Identify a friend of the pricing team, a leader who embraces innovation, experimentation, and exploration. I find that the success of this first project is critical. As this single data point will anchor all future pricing investments and future project deployments, you cannot afford to fail, show unimpressive returns, or disrupt the business. These experiments typically continue until several projects prove successful and pricing leaders can demonstrate a significant, quantifiable return on investment. As much as you may want to undertake a big first project, for operational and political reasons, "baby steps" will get you there faster.

Stage 4. Incremental Adoption

Building on that successful track record, the team extends adoption of the pricing model across the enterprise. This is also a slow process but a surer one. A pilot project can take anywhere from 18 to 24 months. Building a pricing team can take up to 24 months as well. Incremental adoption makes it easier to measure, deliver, and document the overall impact of each project to the C-suite and the pricing council. Incremental adoption reassures the top leaders that pricing programs can affect the bottom line without creating a significant business risk. It also makes it easier to convince the naysayers that advanced pricing works, and skeptics should "prepare to be assimilated," as they say on *Star Trek*. As success stories filter through the organization and the positive noise reaches the C-suite, pricing leaders start preparing the next stage of the road map: enterprise-wide deployment. Only at this point, after seeing multiple successes, are organizational leaders typically ready to entertain a proposal for enterprise-wide pricing program deployment.

Of course, most groups will experience some setbacks at this stage. Not all projects are created equal, nor will they deliver the same results. Failures should not be papered over; it is essential to analyze breakdowns and deviations to account for them and avoid them in subsequent projects. It is therefore critical to carefully select the sequence of projects, how and when they are introduced, and how results are measured, documented, and communicated. Pacing the speed and pace of the project introduction and deployment will be based on the organization's absorption capacity and the quality of the change-management project. Remember that this is more like climbing a mountain than running a race. You can't reach the summit until everything you need has made it to base camp—and if the sherpas aren't sold on the plan, your expedition may not even make it to base camp.

Stage 5. Dynamic Enterprise Integration

At the final stage of the transformation, value and pricing management become embedded in the fabric of the firm. A consensus grows that the impact of pricing is real. At this stage, pricing excellence in the dimensions of pricing orientation and pricing realization have been fully integrated in the firm's DNA and its social fabric. The pace at which new technical resources are integrated can increase, as pricing users become more sophisticated and realize that there is a lot in it for them. Regular upgrades to existing pricing resources and assets begin. The process becomes dynamic. But even more important than these new tools is the attitude toward their adoption: everyone is in favor of them. In Stage 5, the challenge becomes a question of sustaining change over time and of bringing new employees on board fairly quickly. The quality of training and integration is essential. New sales and marketing employees must feel and breathe the corporate priorities right away, including the business model differentiation and the pricing vision.

While I found that most transformations I have witnessed, led, or heard about share these five distinct stages, each transformational journey remains unique in its design and in the nature and pace of its integration of technical pricing capabilities. In addition, three other organizational capabilities are critical in the successful design and deployment of the transformational road map: organizational change, organizational confidence, and executive sponsorship, as shown in Figure 2.3.

As deployed pricing resources become increasingly technical and complex at each stage, the intensity of learning must start high and stay high. Two organizational capabilities associated with pricing—organizational confidence and organizational change capacity—will continue to grow in intensity, as depicted in Figure 2.3. The increase in intensity correlates with

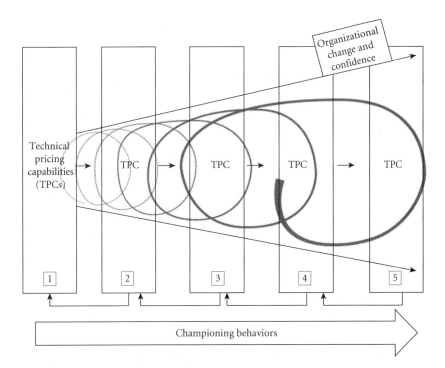

Figure 2.3 Organizational capabilities in the transformation

the increase in organizational scope of the programs as well as their growing complexity. The third organizational capability, related to championing behaviors, will remain constant. Little can be achieved without strong, sustained executive support for the entire project. In fact, champions are critical to overcome the potential—make that almost inevitable—bumps along the transformational journey.

The Bumps Along the Way

This process may sound straightforward, but it only looks that way on a map. From the ground, every pricing transformation is slow and difficult. Whenever I speak to anyone who has led a pricing transformation, I'm struck by two things: first, they always describe it as a journey—and given that the process usually lasts four to ten years, even this metaphor often understates the pain involved—and second, they always add, "and it's not over yet."

The challenges usually begin early, even before you get started with your pricing project. One of the biggest is that the decision to pursue a pricing transformation is made only when some aspect of the company's strategy seems seriously off track. Typically, a pricing project is launched because something is clearly going wrong—margins are eroding, deals require more and more discounting or other kinds of sweeteners, or inventory is piling up. The dilemma is that these pricing problems may just be symptoms of a larger business issue. If that's the case, unless the root causes of these problems are addressed first, the gains made through improved pricing are likely to be limited and of value only for the short term. Before proceeding, you need to be able to answer six questions:

1. *Is our segmentation distinct?* Perhaps the most common marketing problem is a lack of segmentation based on user needs. Without segmentation, firms cannot distinguish between their customers and try to be everything to everyone. The result is customer confusion, severe pricing overlap across segments, and the profit leakages that always occur when customers get things they do not value or are not willing to pay for.

2. *Is our business model robust?* Another significant structural problem that can lead to price erosion is the lack of a sound and differenti-

ated business model. In times of increased competition, business models often face pressure. Before working on their pricing model, managers should examine its strength and decide whether it needs to be somehow changed or reinforced.

3. *Are we considering other business models?* Companies tend to think a lot about product and service innovation and much less about the possibilities for business model innovation. As a result, although they may have significant brainpower tied up in improving offerings and enhancing service, they have no formal mechanism to consider better ways to sell their offering.

4. *Do we have enough differentiation?* Pricing problems are often the result of eroding differentiation. Companies frequently have a weak sense of how their offering compares to the competition and interpret their weakness in the market as a problem with their pricing rather than a problem with their product.

5. *Does our strategy still make sense?* Over time, companies often become too inwardly focused and fail to deliver superior value to their customers. What made for a brilliant strategy in 2004 may be totally out of sync with the market's needs today. Smart pricing can't save a dumb strategy. Sometimes industries and markets experience severe disruptive changes that require the company to make a sharp turn.

6. *Are we strategically aligned?* A pricing problem is often the result of a misalignment between silos. In this situation, the right hand not only does not know what the left hand is doing, it's knocking things out of its grip. The sales force, for example, may not follow the marketing department's plan, or cost accountants may send reports to the sales chief that he chucks immediately into his circular file.

Any discussion regarding the possibility of a pricing transformation should begin here. Generally, these sessions lead to excellent exchanges on business model innovation, value propositions, and the relationship between business strategies and pricing strategies. This isn't an optional reassessment; only when all these questions can be answered positively should you move on to a pricing transformation.

Of course, even after you begin your journey, other nonpricing challenges will arise that may knock your transformation off course. A pricing transformation requires slow and steady work, but modern businesses tend to move in fits and starts. A macroeconomic crisis hits your customers hard. Your industry is going through a round of consolidations. A disruptive innovation by a new competitor weakens your traditional value proposition. Internal challenges may also arise: Key champions of the transformation quit the company, leaving a void. A new CEO takes over, with a different set of strategic priorities, and she starves your unit of the resources needed to make the change. Distracted managers worried about keeping their job beyond the next quarter may be less than patient about investing their political capital on a project that may not pay off for five years. The organization as a whole may sour on the project, particularly if they don't see an immediate gain—and many people will be looking for any excuse to ditch a project that seems to threaten their own power and compensation. In a large organization, your initiative may even face a perfect storm of threats from multiple quarters at the same time.

The 5 Cs of Pricing Transformation

Every firm's pricing journey is different, so chances are good you won't face all of these obstacles—at least not all at once. Firms adopt various pricing resources at different stages, and some stages may be longer or shorter depending on the organization's capacity to change and learn. There is no copy-and-paste template for this process. However, in my research and experience, companies never succeed without five factors that I call "the 5 Cs" (Figure 2.4): champions, center-led management, confidence, change capacity, and pricing capabilities.

This chart may look simple, but it illustrates a model of what it takes to achieve pricing excellence that took me four years to develop. I derived it only after I reviewed the pricing literature, interviewed 44 practitioners at fifteen industrial firms, ran multiple quantitative surveys with over 2,500 respondents, and performed an integrative analysis that I validated through a series of rigorous academic methods. Here's what I found.

Figure 2.4 The 5 Cs of pricing excellence

1. Champions

A progressive pricing orientation is not easy to instill in a company. It tends to be difficult to implement and politically dangerous. For that reason, a pricing transformation almost never happens unless someone at the top, usually the CEO, makes it a priority along with other corporate initiatives.

However, C-suite executives, particularly CEOs, often have no choice but to pursue a fragmented agenda in a highly political environment. They may be influenced by management fads or by particular consultants. They may be overly concerned about maintaining their relationship with the board and staying on the good side of analysts who follow their stock. They may view everything through a limited set of financial key performance indicators (KPIs), such as return on assets (ROA) or Economic Value Added (EVA). In fact, pricing is likely not even a priority. In my survey of CEOs, 66 percent said they do not have a clearly defined pricing vision, 58 percent said they do not have a full-time person managing their prices, and 39 percent admitted they set their prices based on their intuition and experience.

The idea that pricing can be better managed hasn't reached most C-suites yet, in part because it's still little discussed either by business scholars outside the pricing fraternity or in the business press (Liozu and Hinterhuber 2012a). Many CEOs I have spoken to about pricing retain a number of outdated attitudes that keep their organization underperforming. For instance, CEOs of midcap firms tend to think that pricing is important only for large firms with large staffs, and that their own managers do not have the time, staff, or money to take on a major pricing project.

In fact, CEOs do not get involved in pricing at all. My survey found that they are much more focused on cost reduction programs and growth initiatives than price management. Pricing runs a distant third as a topic for CEOs, far behind cost and growth. They claim it takes on average only 16 percent of their attention—and that is probably overstating the case. Typically, CEOs delegate pricing management to the chief marketing officer, the chief financial officer, or the vice president of sales. Nor do these officers do much; without C-suite and CEO support, their pricing program is unlikely to succeed. Middle managers won't necessarily feel obliged to support the new program. Tensions, conflicts, and power struggles are more likely to crop up, and resources may be cut off or diverted long before the transformation takes root.

Even if the CEO does take an interest in pricing and tries to maintain some level of involvement—discussing margins, reviewing strategic contracts, meeting with large accounts, and approving pricing conditions for long-term agreements—the focus is still not likely to be sufficient for a successful transformation. As one executive warned me, "Make sure that top management does support the initial rollout . . . because the rollout is critical." Another executive, looking back on his company's successful pricing transformation, said one key was "definitely the fact that top management helped sell it, helped, honestly, push it along as well . . . without the top management, it wouldn't have happened."

The buck starts here! If the pricing program is to succeed, the CEO must champion the transformation. She must sell the vision and the strategy to her key internal stakeholders, find the resources to dedicate to the long-term transformation, and even sit in at all pricing-related meetings. She should celebrate any heroes of the pricing initiative and fete them with awards, recognition, and a lunch. She should read, review, and comment on pricing reports, and include information on value and pricing as part of the annual report and other corporate communications. She should add a chief pricing officer to the C-suite and, perhaps most importantly, back up sales during difficult price negotiations.

But the CEO isn't the only possible champion. Pricing champions are useful wherever they are found on the org chart. For nearly 50 years, management theorists have known that a champion can make all the difference in the successful adoption of a technological change. Fifty years ago, Donald Schön, a Massachusetts Institute of Technology scholar studying radical military innovation (1963), first identified the role of champions in propagating innovation in an organization. Schön found that organizations succeeded in their adoption of new technologies only when a champion was willing to "promote ideas actively and vigorously through informal networks and to risk his or her position and prestige to ensure the innovation success" (Schön 1963). He concluded that a new idea "either finds a champion or dies." Chakrabarti (1974) later observed that a champion plays a critical role at all stages in overcoming technical and organizational obstacles and often succeeds through the "sheer force of his will and energy."

2. Center-Led Management

Decentralized pricing has some advantages, including the ability to give the sales force a maximum degree of pricing flexibility and the ability to apply some creativity in designing a deal. However, decentralized pricing has several serious disadvantages too. As one executive at a company that used decentralized pricing told me, pricing at his company tends to be a "judgment call . . . not a written-down process." With a decentralized pricing structure, headquarters is likely to find it harder to enforce corporate pricing programs, and in extreme cases, the enterprise as a whole may leak revenue because of rogue discounting.

A centralized design, on the other hand, comes with its own set of trade-offs. On the plus side, the price leaders in a centralized system have more control and are better able to reduce cost. They can set rules that keep the whole system in line with their goals. On the minus side, centralized pricing can be more labor intensive, and the sales force may be frustrated by their low flexibility. Their nonresponsiveness may lead some salespeople to describe their pricing group as "the sales prevention department." Their rules may also fail to account for some important intangibles that are not reflected on a standardized pricing sheet.

Fortunately, there is a third alternative: the center-led team. Center-led teams try to combine the advantages of both models in a single entity. This group of pricing experts works closely with the people in the field who have direct insight into consumer behavior. Almost all of the value-based pricing organizations I have studied have a center-led pricing capability run by experts who typically lead a formal review process before making any decision.

3. Pricing Capabilities

The third C is pricing capabilities. A company that has advanced pricing skills and systems can respond quickly to market changes, knows its competitors' pricing tactics, and does an effective job in pricing its product and services has most of the capabilities it needs to be a pricing leader. Three different surveys of professional pricing experts (Professional Pricing Society), chief executive officers (Young Presidents' Organization), and senior salespeople (Strategic Account Management Association) all show a high correlation between advanced pricing capabilities and the profit of the firm. In fact, between 34 and 66 percent of a firm's pricing performance may be traced to the strength of its pricing capabilities. Those capabilities include training a variety of sales and marketing people on pricing and the development of business intelligence, market research, pricing research, and proprietary tools to capture and quantify customer value. Pricing capabilities thus include both tangible and intangible resources and assets that get deployed in the firm to support the transformational agenda.

4. Change Capacity

Software and consulting companies sometimes give the impression that advanced pricing capabilities can simply be bolted on to your other processes. In fact, customer value-based pricing requires constant and ongoing adjustments in the organization, not just as the new system is implemented but even after the company reaches Stage 5 and value-based pricing has gone company-wide.

Not everybody is able to make the transition. As one vice president of global sales and marketing at a company embarked on a pricing journey told us:

> We put people on performance reviews . . . the guy who was number one in targeted attainment three years ago was number three in sales target attainment last year . . . And he's on performance plan right now. The reason he's on a performance plan is because he's at the bottom of the barrel on [value selling]. . . . We said to him, "This isn't acceptable. I can get anyone to look after the [equipment] side. What I need someone is to change the market." . . . We've released a couple of people who haven't been able to make the transition, which has been difficult . . . That kind of performance management alignment is key.

A company with a strong capacity for change usually has a lot going right for it: capable and trustworthy leaders, trusting followers, and mid-level managers who are good at linking senior executives with the rest of the organization. The company has an innovative culture that is at the same time accountable and effective, and its management can solve problems by zeroing in on root causes.

5. Confidence

Pricing problems often stem from a lack of confidence. You may see it in erratic discounting behaviors by the sales force: sales reps who begin offering discounts a nanosecond after negotiations begin or who let the customer stipulate a host of new terms and conditions. A sales frenzy brought on by an end-of-the-quarter discount may be a bad sign as well. You'll also get a hint of insecurity if R&D, marketing, and sales all speak different pricing languages. If R&D speaks innovation, marketing speaks value, and sales talks about discounts, chances are good that the company doesn't have the degree of shared conviction about the value of its offerings that a company needs to make its prices stick.

In my qualitative interviews, I found that a company with a successful pricing approach tends to have a "can do" attitude that materializes as follows: it has courage—the courage to resist customer objections and to increase prices when needed, and the courage to stand firm when faced with customer pressures (Liozu and Hinterhuber 2012b). Sales reps need to think like the models in the L'Oréal ad: You pay more "because I'm worth it." As one executive told us, "You have to look [customers] in the eye and say, 'Ours costs more. This costs more, and it's worth it. You should pay more for that.' You have to be pretty confident to do that."

A number of factors tend to enhance this sense of confidence. In my discussions with companies that have adopted value-based pricing, sales-people tend to have a high level of confidence not only in their company's offering but also in its price-setting intelligence. Much of this confidence comes down to resilience; a resilient company can analyze its failures, learn from them, and improve. Managers at a resilient company tend to persevere with their pricing transformation even if an individual initiative fails, and they have learned how to cope with uncertainty. Coaching and superior talent management adds confidence as well. Coaching the sales force, creating incentive programs geared toward value and pricing excellence, and com-municating positive messages can all help keep spirits high.

It also doesn't hurt to know you're right. Happy talk can only go so far; what will really convince the reps is when they see several pilot pricing projects succeed. Most of all, some executives say you have to have a strong belief in your offering as a premium product. The people inside need to "believe that what you're doing is better than the next guy, that you're us-ing better ingredients, that you have better technology behind the product formulation, that you can—the product consistently has to be there," one executive told me.

As these 5 Cs suggest, pricing can't simply be "adopted," as many author-ities have taught (Liozu, Hinterhuber, Perelli, et al. 2012). Instead, imple-mentation and internalization of technical pricing resources and activities requires deep organizational changes, and these changes transform the fab-ric of the firm. Value-based pricing often entails changes throughout the enterprise, because it demands a dispassionate, objective look at the value the company creates from the customer's point of view—and not infre-quently, what the customer cares about and what the company previously considered the core value of its offering are somewhat different things.

Instead of a quick fix, the implementation of advanced and progressive pricing requires a slow mutation of the firm's DNA from cost or competition to customer value. It is a long and sometimes painful evolution for the organization and its actors. The process requires an intense and sustained organizational mobilization to transform established structure, culture, processes, and systems. Marketers, sellers, and developers have to change their frames of reference and embrace new value-related concepts as a new "way of life" (Forbis and Mehta 1981). They also must learn a new language in order to carry the value message internally and externally. As one executive I interviewed told me, several years into his company's transformation:

> It's a journey. It's a journey with multiple, multiple small steps, and [we have] been on this journey for a while. A lot of progress was made, but the journey is not complete. We've got a ways to go . . .

Conclusion

Over the past few years, I have made multiple presentations of my 5C model. The model resonates in particular with pricing practitioners who are not making any significant progress in their transformation process. These pricing practitioners had managed to get large investments in pricing approved but ended up fighting strong organizational internal resistance and headwinds. They were faced with a lack of collective confidence in teams to complete programs. To find out what went wrong, I walked them through the 5C model and asked them to tell me how they had used each of the Cs. It turned out that all of them had at least two Cs and generally three Cs missing—most frequently champions, change management, and confidence.

Another way to think of this journey is as a process of acquiring new analytical left-brain skills and softer right-brain skills. Pricing is a quantitative task in the end and requires superior left-brain capabilities in analytics, modeling, and software expertise. At the same time, however, it won't be adopted without leaders who know how to build teams and collaborate, who can be influential without necessarily having direct authority, and who have good storytelling and conversational skills. Leave out either hemisphere and your pricing initiative will stall. Neglect the left brain on the first steps and you won't have the data or the analytical capabilities you need; neglect the right brain in the latter stages, as you try to convert the company to value-based pricing, and you will also fail. Only by cultivating your organization's capacities for both left- and right-brained skills can your company succeed with pricing.

Over the next five chapters, we will look at each of the *Cs* in more detail and their contributions to a pricing transformation—why they are so important, how they function, how to integrate them into your company's pricing practices, and, most importantly, how to start developing them.

3 Champions
Leading the Organizational Mobilization

People make their choices about where to focus based on their perception of what matters to leaders.

Daniel Goleman, *Focus: The Hidden Driver of Excellence*

People often ask me if the CEO needs to be involved in a pricing transformation. Chief executives live under extraordinary time constraints and must juggle so many obligations that the last thing they need is one more number-one priority. Couldn't someone in finance or marketing take it on?

Unfortunately, I have a simple answer: no. In my experience, not only does the CEO need to be involved, the CEO needs to champion the adoption and assimilation of every aspect and every stage of the transformation. In the 5C model, the champion is perhaps the most critical C of all. To put it bluntly, unless the CEO makes it clear that pricing is a top priority, the pricing transformation won't happen. Or if it does happen, the pace will be exceedingly slow. But if a CEO pays attention to pricing literature, he shouldn't require too much persuasion; a 2012 survey by Simon-Kucher & Partners suggests that after a CEO gets involved in pricing strategy, pricing power tends to increase by 35 percent. I can't put a number to it yet, but my research also indicates that CEOs have a critical role to play.

Why should that be? I'm a big rugby fan and to me, a company that succeeds in a pricing transformation is kind of like a winning rugby team. To an outsider, a rugby match looks like a bunch of big lugs piling on top of each other, interrupted by the occasional lucky pass. Force and luck do play a role in rugby, as in anything, but if you look closely, you'll also find logic, strategy, and artistry. Most of all, you will find that the ball never gets over the goal line without courage and teamwork, inspired by a leader with the stamina to keep running and tackling for 80 minutes with one 10-minute break. As Thierry Dusautoir, the captain of Stade Toulousain, my home-town rugby team, likes to say: "I lead by example by going to battle and ask my team to join me."

A company transformation to pricing excellence is like that. From the outside, you'll see enough moving parts that the process charts look like arms and legs locked in a tight scrum. But from the inside, all the action re-flects a clear and definite plan driven by an organizational champion. Until a year or two ago, this was just my intuition based on my experience and anecdotes collected in various books and at pricing conferences, but more recent research now suggests that a pricing transformation goes nowhere fast unless the CEO is willing to get out on the field and fight like Thierry Dusautoir.

However, you will only be able to fight that hard if you believe in the cause. As a pricing champion, you will need to begin by taking stock of your perceptions about pricing. Many executives believe in a variety of pricing myths—later in this book, I devote a whole chapter to pricing myths—and it holds their organizations back. People in the organization pay attention to what their leaders say about pricing, so if you don't believe in it, they won't either.

CEOs' Perceptions of Pricing

By and large, CEOs understand that pricing can be a strategic lever of prof-itability, helpful for both gross and operating margins. My research shows that most CEOs see pricing as a priority for their business and say that they have seen its potential impact in other firms (Table 3.1). This may sound like most C-suites are busy with pricing projects. In fact, this is not the case. As I noted in the last chapter, when asked to divide 100 points of attention between cost cutting, growth, and pricing programs, CEOs said that pricing received only 16 percent of their attention—and that was the average.

Among the 557 CEOs surveyed, evidence suggests that most have not invested much in the way of time and resources on pricing:

- 66 percent have not clearly identified a pricing vision.
- 58 percent do not have a full-time person managing prices.

Table 3.1 CEOs' perceptions of pricing

CEOs understand the power of pricing			
CEOs' perceptions of pricing (1 = strongly disagree to 7 = strongly agree)	Total (n = 557)	Manufacturing (n = 218)	Service (n = 210)
Strategic pricing can increase profitability.	6.29	6.31	6.27
My employees actively engage in the pricing process.	5.36	5.42	5.36
I have seen what other companies can achieve with pricing.	5.08	**4.85**	5.27
Our current gross margins are satisfactory.	3.98	3.89	4.00
It is difficult to demonstrate the return on investment for pricing programs (scale reversed).	3.42	3.33	3.57
Pricing is not a top priority for us right now (scale reversed).	2.29	**2.06**	**2.49**

. . . but the crisis requires a different focus			
Allocation of 100 points of attention	Total (n = 557)	Manufacturing (n = 218)	Service (n = 210)
Variable- and fixed-cost reduction programs	54%	**52%**	**57%**
Growth initiatives	30%	**33%**	**27%**
Price management programs	16%	15%	16%
	100%	100%	100%

NOTE: Bold numbers are significantly different at the 95% confidence interval.

- 38 percent have not identified a pricing strategy.
- 39 percent say they set prices based on intuition and experience.

The bottom line is that most CEOs do not pay much attention to pricing. When they do get around to it, they tend to be too late or have to do it as part of a painful restructuring. They are usually more reactive than proactive as they are pulled in so many directions.

So how do you get your CEO to pay more attention? It's a challenge; unlike most other critical functions, pricing has no natural advocate in the C-suite. To get a message in the ear of the CEO, you will need to find a true believer in pricing with a seat at the table. Generally speaking, the chief marketing officer and the chief financial officer are the executives best equipped to carry a strong message upstream, but you'll have to persuade them first—and even the most persuasive C-suite member probably won't get far until he can show the results of some successful pilot projects. Success is critical. But creating a buzz about success is even more important. During Stages 2 and 3 of the transformational model, quick wins and

About the Research

Following the total design method (Dillman, Smyth, and Christian 2009), a cross-sectional self-administered electronic survey was sent to 7,897 active members of the Young Presidents' Organization (YPO) in April 2011. YPO is a for-profit organization with 22,000 business owner/executive members in 125 countries. Members of YPO must meet eligibility criteria, such as age (under 45 years old), title (president, chief executive officer, chairman of the board, managing director, and/or managing partner), enterprise value (minimum $10 million USD), number of employees (minimum 50) and annual sales revenues (minimum $8 million for sales, service, and manufacturing corporations; $160 million for financial institutions; and $6 million for agency-type businesses). To my knowledge, no other empirical studies have used the YPO database.

The survey was emailed to 7,897 targeted respondents, of which 376 were returned for reasons of email discrepancies. Of the remaining 7,521 surveys, 902 were returned partially or fully completed for a response rate of 12 percent. I deemed 557 surveys usable for analysis. The response rate is consistent with the surveys of other top executives (Simsek, Heavey, and Veiga 2010; Hambrick, Geletkanycz, and Fredrickson 1993).

Eighty percent of the responding firms identified themselves as manufacturing or service firms, with the remaining classified as retail/distribution firms. Over half

success stories have to find their way into the C-suite. This is why having an ally in the boardroom is important; if the CEO isn't sold, your initiative is unlikely to get very far. Here's why.

Pricing Champions and Transformational Leadership

Several studies have examined pricing practices from the perspective of organizational decision processes, but only a handful link pricing and organizational behavior. One of those studies was mine (Liozu et al. 2011). In my study, I found that in firms that used some form of cost-based pricing, almost all executives had limited involvement with the pricing function. Their contribution was limited to approval of unusual price deviations, input on large contract negotiations, clarification of uncertain or ambiguous

(61 percent) were B2B firms vs. B2C (39 percent). About 11 percent were publicly traded, while 87 percent reported being privately owned. Seventy-three percent indicated they owned the firm. Half (50 percent) had fewer than 250 employees, 22 percent had 251 to 500 employees, 13 percent had 501 to 1,000 employees, and 15 percent had more than 1,000 employees (3 percent had more than 10,000 employees). Fifty-three percent reported the age of their firm as older than 10 years but less than 50 years. Thirty-four percent indicated their firm had been in business for longer than 50 years.

A six-item scale adapted from Howell, Shea, and Higgins (2005) was used to assess pricing champion behaviors. Each item was measured using a seven-point Likert scale anchored at the extremes by "strongly disagree" and "strongly agree."

To what extent do you agree or disagree with the following statements about your involvement with pricing? (1 = strongly disagree to 7 = strongly agree)

1. I enthusiastically promote the pricing function.
2. I express confidence in what pricing can do.
3. I show tenacity in overcoming obstacles when changes in pricing are needed.
4. I get pricing problems into the hands of those who can solve them.
5. I get key decision makers involved in the pricing process.
6. I act as a champion of pricing.

prices, and the conduct of general business reviews. Top management in these firms tended to be involved only in day-to-day and tactical pricing issues. By contrast, I found that all of the executives in firms that used value-based pricing had actively engaged in championing its implementation. Managers characterized these executives as driving the internalization of value-based pricing throughout the firm and motivating the organizational changes needed to support it. Of course, correlation is not causation, but the fact that, among the companies I interviewed, five out of six sales and marketing managers who had adopted value-based pricing told me that they felt the support and conviction of top managers was an essential part of pricing adoption suggests to me that my intuition is correct.

The reason CEO championing is so important has to do with how decisions are made within companies. Top management plays a key role not only in defining and promoting corporate-wide priorities and new strategic programs but also in identifying, allocating, and deploying strategic resources to support these programs (Chandler 1973:4). This is also true of pricing, in a negative sense; in the absence of executive direction, prices tend to be set internally, by consensus between departments. Cyert and March (1992), two of the most reputable behavioral scientists to have studied pricing behaviors in a retail environment, suggested 20 years ago that most decisions are made by rules of thumb that emerge within the firm over time. They argue that in the case of pricing, prices are negotiated between various departments of the firm as a way to reach consensus. They list cost-based pricing as one of those mental shortcuts.

Lancioni, Schau, and Smith (2005) researched intraorganizational influences on business-to-business pricing strategies, particularly the impact of interdepartmental rivalry and conflicting internal interests on the pricing process. They found that resistance to progressive pricing strategies emanates from many groups within the firm, each of which has its own set of parochial interests and agendas. The biggest objections tend to be raised by the finance department, but Lancioni also pointed a finger at senior managers generally because of their desire to control the process.

Ironically, however, lack of pricing information is probably one reason for their resistance; it's natural to want to hit the brakes when driving through fog. Ingenbleek (2007) conducted a meta-analysis of 53 pricing studies drawn from cost-principle theory, decision-making theory, and marketing strategy and found that many firms' pricing policies suffered because the leaders did not have the data they needed to reach a decision.

As this prior research suggests, part of the problem CEOs face is that in the beginning of a pricing transformation, they tend to find themselves caught in a bind; lack of a pricing orientation in the company usually means that no one in the C-suite knows anything about pricing, and because they haven't focused on pricing, they never made gathering pricing data a priority. No knowledge and no data make it difficult for CEOs to understand the return on investment (ROI) of pricing, and without a clear sense of the ROI, they're reluctant to invest time and money in an expensive initiative.

They have also had few places to turn for more insight. Business schools have made surprisingly little effort to break this cycle of ignorance. Until recently, marketing and pricing scholars have been almost silent about both the consequences of pricing orientations on overall company performance (Cressman 1999; Ingenbleek 2007; Hinterhuber 2008b) and on how value-based pricing may lead to superior firm performance.

But this is one scrum the CEO needs to win.

First, the potential rewards are huge. As I demonstrated earlier in the book, designing and executing a modern pricing approach to pricing can raise margins by as much as 2 percent—an enormous win in a billion-dollar company.

Second, companies where the CEOs act as pricing champions have a funny way of turning into champions themselves—and for the same reason that Thierry Dusautoir, the best rugby player in the world, just happens to be the captain of the best rugby team in the world. In a survey I conducted of 557 members of the Young Presidents' Organization, a group of chief executives under 45 years old who run enterprises worth at least $10 million, we found strong links between having a pricing champion in the top job, organizational design, and relative firm performance. Nor am I alone in this conclusion; a 2012 study of 40 companies by Deloitte found that participating companies identified as high performers are nearly twice as likely as low performers to have a C-level executive involved in pricing.

Third, merely believing that strategic pricing works seems to be an important predictor of profitability. My survey found that a CEO's belief in pricing correlated more strongly with profitability than the amount of time she allocated to cost-cutting programs. Of course, walking the talk mattered too; the amount of time the CEO spent on pricing management programs also correlated closely with profitability.

In fact, it's difficult to read the data in any other way than to conclude that the degree to which the CEO acts as a pricing champion is an extremely important predictor of pricing power (Liozu and Hinterhuber 2012a).

So how does a CEO become a pricing champion? What does that mean exactly, and if your CEO is just vaguely supportive now, how can you convince him to join your huddle?

Constellation of Champion Behaviors in Pricing

The first step is to see whether your CEO has what it takes to lead such a transformation. Transformational leaders achieve their magic by practicing a "constellation of behaviors" (Howell, Shea, and Higgins 2005), including "communicating a clear vision of what innovation could be or do, displaying enthusiasm and demonstrating commitment to it, and involving others in supporting it" (Howell and Higgins 1990).

Scholars say that six behaviors are most crucial (Figure 3.1):

- *Enthusiasm.* The level of optimism and energy shown when engaging teams involved in the various pricing projects and initiatives
- *Conviction.* The degree of conviction and resilience shown during good and difficult times of the change journey
- *Charisma.* Leading with passion, power, and persuasive words to inspire employees to embark in the pricing transformation
- *Confidence.* Showing resilience, creating a vision that people can adopt, and generating ongoing buy-in the pricing transformation
- *Attention.* Being present, visible, and active during specific activities of the various pricing projects

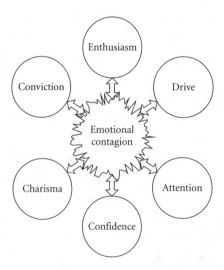

Figure 3.1 Championing behaviors

- *Drive.* Pushing the organization, reinforcing the need for change, and, if necessary, getting directly involved in more difficult or slower projects to make them move forward

A deficiency in some of these behaviors should be no cause for concern. Your CEO will undoubtedly have at least some of them at her disposal—the meek may inherit the earth, but they don't generally make it to the corner office. However, if your CEO is as charismatic as a table and lacks most of these behaviors, don't give up. Behavioral scholars describe a constellation of behaviors, not traits; you're stuck with traits, but behaviors can be learned. Over time, with coaching and a deep understanding of the pricing issues, some of those shortcomings can be overcome. Where gaps can't be filled, the CEO may be able to delegate some of the emotional cheerleading to another executive if the selected executive has a high level of credibility and if employees believe that the CEO is behind the initiative 100 percent.

This behavior really can be learned. I know; I have conducted several pricing transformation projects myself, and I can tell you that with practice, you can get better. I was hardly Mr. Motivation in my first pricing transformation, but I've improved since then. In my latest job, as a CEO, I had raised the level of my game enough that I was able to call myself the chief energizing officer and not get laughed out of the room. I don't think my case is exceptional. With enough passion, most CEOs can lead teams through difficult times, challenging projects, and transformational initiatives. Becoming a pricing champion is a choice, not a destiny—just like pricing leadership.

Top Management Involvement Versus Championing

Most management involves nudges and pats—a little encouragement, a word of warning, and employees will go off and do their best to meet the company's goals. A pricing transformation is an exception. Without strong executive support, pricing revolutions tend to lose momentum (Figure 3.2). Strong middle managers will do everything they can to block progress of such an initiative, even if the workers at the bottom and the top managers are both convinced of the need to make a change. When that happens, organizational confidence and buy-in evaporate. Other programs win attention

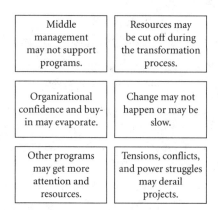

Middle management may not support programs.	Resources may be cut off during the transformation process.
Organizational confidence and buy-in may evaporate.	Change may not happen or may be slow.
Other programs may get more attention and resources.	Tensions, conflicts, and power struggles may derail projects.

Figure 3.2 What may happen without the CEO's attention

and resources, making it easier for support to be cut off during the transformation. The pace of change slows down, power struggles and conflicts rise, and gradually your transformation slows down, wobbles, and stops.

To drive a transformation forward, the leader must make it clear that she does not see the initiative as an interesting experiment. No one can be under the illusion it's one of those short-lived C-suite enthusiasms middle managers can dodge until executive interest burns out.

But even that won't be enough. The CEO needs to champion the cause, not just be involved. For the involved CEO, pricing can be treated as just one more box in a long list of boxes to be ticked, like a commendable but low-priority HR initiative. An involved CEO will discuss margins, review strategic contracts and meet with large accounts, approve pricing conditions for long-term agreements, react to price erosion, and push for price increases. Occasionally, she may even visit the pricing council. The commitment is real, but the investment is still too limited to lead to a genuine transformation. Such an investment is still likely to leave the company "a day late and a dollar short."

A CEO who intends to champion a price transformation needs to make the initiative a core part of the job and see the creation of a price-conscious culture as a core part of her legacy (Figure 3.3). This leader will need to develop a strong corporate pricing vision, strategy, and organization; ensure proper resource allocation to support long-term projects; sponsor the pric-

Figure 3.3 CEO's championing versus involvement

ing council and attend all its meetings; focus on building long-term pricing capabilities; and show commitment to pricing with dedicated championing behaviors.

Championing requires active engagement, active listening, a proactive interest in value and pricing matters, and most of all a lot more sweat equity. True championing means grand gestures—traveling with the sales force to visit difficult accounts, to negotiate complex contracts, or to announce a large price increase. Sharing the pain with the people in the front line shows that the CEO cares and is willing to lead by example. By taking actions in the front line, she becomes a true hero in the eyes of the organization.

Being a champion takes a lot of time and effort. It requires courage to face the resistance of top and middle managers, especially when some of the pricing programs require dramatic change and tough decisions. So why bother? Just one reason: it works. My research suggests that if a CEO can transform her pricing culture, not only can she give her company greater profitability than the average company in its industry, but through smarter market segmentation, the company will be able to serve its customers better. This isn't a zero-sum game, like some working capital exercises. At the end of the process, both customer and company will be better off.

Over and over again in the course of my research, I heard that top management support made all the difference in driving a pricing transformation. "The fact that top management was behind [the pricing implementation]—that was probably the critical piece that made it successful," one pricing executive told me, reflecting on what had gone right with their rollout.

"What made [value-based pricing] work was, looking back, definitely the fact that top management helped sell it, helped, honestly, push it along as well . . . without the top management, it wouldn't have happened," said another executive at another firm.

Talk to anyone you know at a firm with a working pricing system and I can practically guarantee that you will hear the same thing. In fact, I hear this systematically at every single price-related conference. At two recent pricing conferences, one in New York City and one in Cannes, France, I saw presentations on a number of companies' pricing transformations, including Arrow, HP, and Gates International, and I heard again and again that the C-suite and the top champions were crucial to the success of their journey.

The Role of Mindful Champions

Beyond simply making sure the initiative's blockers are shoved aside, the participation of CEOs and other senior executives in a pricing transformation generally has a number of other positive cultural effects. Acting in the role of mindful champions, such committed senior executives serve as important role models in improving the organization's degree of decision-making rationality, collective mindfulness, and pricing orientation.

Decision-Making Rationality

Over 50 years ago, Simon (1961:93) found that managers' decisions tend to fall short of objective rationality in three ways: (1) they acted without full knowledge of the issue they were deciding; (2) they failed to anticipate the consequences that would follow their choice; and (3) they favored one choice among all possible alternative behaviors without considering alternatives. Their abilities are compromised too because like the rest of us, they suffer from a "bottleneck of attention" that limits their ability to deal with more than a few things at a time (Simon 1961:90). Most of us live with bounded rationality, significantly constrained by limitations of information and calculation (Cyert and March 1992:214).

Behavioral theorists conjecture that managers in organizations simplify the decision-making process by using various behaviors (Cyert and March 1992:264), such as "satisficing" (March 1978), following rules of thumb (Schwenk 1988), and defining standard operating procedures and organizational routines (Pentland and Reuter 1994; Feldman 2000). Others define frames of reference (March, Simon, and Guetzkow 1958:159) that can be determined "by the limitations of the rational man's knowledge." Experienced managers draw from their memory, training, and experience (Simon 1961:134). They construct and use "cognitive heuristics" (Brownlie and Spender 1995) or mental models (Porac, Thomas, and Baden-Fuller 1989) to simplify complex strategic issues and engage in intuitive and judgmental responses to situations that demand decisions (Barnard and Andrews 1968; Oxenfeldt 1973). They try to "to create a rationality, a recipe or an interpretative scheme" (Brownlie and Spender 1995) that leads to a choice or a decision.

Collective Mindfulness

Originally characterized by Langer (1989) as a state of alertness present in active information processing, mindfulness really means learning to look at problems with a fresh eye. A mindful executive will create new categories rather than rely on categories present in our memory, welcome new information by being open and attentive to changed signals, and invite multiple interpretations. Fiol and O'Connor (2003:60) observe that "the greater the level of mindfulness of decision makers, the more likely it is they will use decision-making mechanisms to expand their search for information." Weick, Sutcliffe, and Obstfeld (1999) extended the concept of individual mindfulness (Langer 1989, 1997) to the group, describing it as the widespread adoption and diffusion of mindfulness by the organization's members. Mindfulness helps organizations notice more issues, process them with care, and detect and respond to early signs of trouble (Weick and Sutcliffe 2007).

As with championing, mindfulness can be broken into a number of smaller components, all of which can also be nurtured. Weick and Sutcliffe (2007; Weick et al. 1999) describe five cognitive processes that constitute organizational mindfulness: (1) preoccupation with failure, (2) reluctance to simplify interpretations, (3) sensitivity to operations, (4) commitment to resilience, and (5) deference to expertise. These characteristics of deeply mindful organizations can also be applied to the adoption and implementation of pricing strategies. The CEO must be convinced about the importance of adding organizational mindfulness as a critical competency and work to make it part of the company's repertoire.

Although it's difficult to be steadily mindful, it's not hard to begin. The CEO can make sure failures are analyzed, understood, and celebrated. She should engage the front-line salespeople, who face pricing pressure on a daily basis, and test the pulse of all the front-line employees to make sure the pricing journey stays relevant at every level of the organization. Pricing mindfulness at the organizational level also means learning from the pricing models used in other industries and picking up positive pricing signals that may lead to success. It may also mean that changes in pricing strategy are tested carefully and mindfully before they are implemented. Think of the pricing changes Netflix and JCPenney attempted to make in their respective markets; were the CEOs mindful to the potential risk of failure? Were they paying enough attention to detail? Probably not.

In my survey of CEOs and company presidents, I found that a purposeful championing of pricing activities by top executives strongly influences the firm's organizational design to support the pricing process in five critical areas (decision making, rationality, collective mindfulness, capabilities, and pricing orientation). All relationships between championing behaviors and other organizational characteristics were positive and significant. The survey results also showed that pricing capabilities are influenced by these championing behaviors, and that capabilities tend to enhance firm performance against competitors.

But this doesn't mean that the CEO should micromanage the revolution; Dutta et al. (2002:66) say that "most CEOs will never set a single price. They can, however, give their managers the ability to win price wars, maintain price leadership and hold a competitive edge in pricing."

Conclusion: Upward Price Management

Middle managers who are convinced of the importance of pricing often tell me that their pricing initiatives are going nowhere fast because they lack

Figure 3.4 The power of a pricing champion

senior management support, and they ask me what they should do to get it. I always tell them that the first thing to be done is to show them the data. The proof is in the pudding! And not only their own results; a growing number of studies and consulting reports prove that pricing works and that pricing technology investments tend to have a spectacular ROI. Next, I say, set up a pilot. Once you can prove to your CEO that it works, you're much more likely to make a convert.

I have spent the last six years studying the field of pricing and its impact on organizations. Over and over again, I have found that the combination of advanced pricing systems, progressive and modern pricing capabilities, and a CEO championing the pricing journey all positively and significantly improve firm performance, as depicted in Figure 3.4. Building these technical and social capabilities is a question of unique organizational design that creates organizational capital in pricing and leads to superior and inimitable competitive advantage. My experience and my research both suggest that a pricing transformation is not only worth the trouble of convincing the CEO of its merits, it's worth the trouble of persuading the CEO to champion. It's not easy, but success seldom is. As my fellow rugby players like to say, "Victory is the prize. Pain is the price."

Champions: Some Tips to Get Started

1. Identify a member of the C-suite who may be receptive to the pricing story. Strengthen this alliance by promoting pricing successes in his department.

2. Discuss with your superior how you could secure some time in front of top management to present the case for making a pricing journey or to showcase the results of a pilot.

3. If you have a pricing council, use it to promote specific pricing successes. Positive "noise" raises visibility.

4. Be ready to justify your work with a one- or two-minute elevator speech if you happen to meet the CEO as part of a formal meeting or informally in the cafeteria.

5. Measure the impact of pricing on a quarterly basis and make sure these metrics are communicated widely.

4 Center-Led Price Management

A Hybrid Organizational Architecture for Pricing

To reverse the old U.S. Army recruitment slogan, a transformational pricing journey is not just an adventure, it's a job. A lot of practical details need to be thought through for the project to succeed: To whom should pricing report? How do we organize the pricing function now that we are putting pricing as one of the priorities? Where should the pricing authority reside? Many of these questions logically require top leadership discussions and decisions. The CEO will probably even have to get involved, to make sure the pricing function is positioned at the right place within the organization to ensure transformational success.

Organizational design for the pricing transformation will be an ongoing discussion throughout the journey. Even with a strong commitment at the top and enthusiasm at the bottom, steady pricing discipline can be difficult to maintain year after year. Push too hard from the top and people rebel. Push too lightly and bad old discounting habits will slowly creep back. In fact, the only approach I have found that seems to make it possible to inject sophisticated pricing practices into a company's DNA permanently is our second *C*, a structure I call center-led price management.

This *C* is not for everyone. The "best" organizational structure for your company will depend on the dynamics of your industry, the type of competition you face in the marketplace, and your firm's internal organization. For example, if you work in a firm with a centralized culture, chances are good that the pricing process should be centralized. The preferences and experiences of the CEO and/or the top pricing leader should also be considered. I recently interviewed a vice president of pricing for a large industrial conglomerate who told me he would not decentralize pricing authority under any circumstances. And he may be making the right decision for his company; at the end of the day, there are no absolute rights or wrongs in pricing organization. The important thing is to build a system that has an architecture that reflects the firm's current level of pricing maturity but also takes into account the pricing challenges it faces.

What the Literature Is Telling Us

"Organizing is one of the central and inescapable tasks of top management. And the experienced executive is painfully aware of how little is known as to what constitutes effective organization" (Simon et al. 1954:iii). From that conclusion, reached by Herbert A. Simon in 1954 on the trade-offs of centralization versus decentralization, to the recent *McKinsey Quarterly* issue on the same topic (Campbell, Kunisch, and Muller-Stewens 2011), the debate on how to organize functional teams has raged on and on, with still no end in sight. And these guys are nearly a hundred years ahead of pricing scholars; pricing academics haven't even started to ask questions about how organizational and behavioral characteristics of firms may affect pricing processes (Ingenbleek 2007).

Centralization Versus Decentralization

Management literature is rich in papers and studies for and against centralization. The controversy goes all the way back to the 1920s, when large multinational corporations first evaluated organizational-design options (Cummings 1995). The debate has raged on ever since, though in the late 1940s, some scholars began to demand a truce. Fayol (1949:33) tried to split the difference, stating that "the question of centralization or decentralization is simply a matter of proportion; it is a matter of finding the optimum degree for the particular concern." More recently, scholars have suggested that hybrid organizations and behaviors may be an appropriate intermediate design between polar forms of centralization (Argyres and Silverman 2004). Additionally, for companies coping with organizational change and the difficult adoption and implementation of technology, some theorists have suggested that organizational structures may sometimes need to evolve as the enterprise grows (Hall 1977:215). Hall argues that a centralized approach may be more appropriate for the initial implementation stage to ensure organizational buy-in, whereas a more decentralized approach may be better once the changes are internalized and adoption levels are high.

More recently, change theorists have characterized the centralized-versus-decentralized phenomenon as a "pendulum swing" whose speed is dictated by the external environment (Evaristo, Desouza, and Hollister 2005:67), or dismissed those shifts as a "fashion that is inherently temporary," driven by management gurus (Cummings 1995:116). The focus has now moved back to the question of operating effectiveness first raised by Simon and colleagues (1954:21), of gain-versus-pain analysis (Campbell, Kunisch, and Muller-Stewens 2011), and of the creation of competitive advantage through unique organizational design (Dutta et al. 2002).

Delegation of Pricing Authority

The question of how much pricing authority to delegate to the sales organization also rages on. Like the centralization conundrum, whether to delegate decision-making authority to the sales force is a difficult and emotional question that can have dire consequences if not managed well. Typically, the sales function claims they have the deepest understanding of the customers' pricing behavior and should make the final price decision (Lancioni, Schau, and Smith 2005), but top management and the finance function think the reps are too willing to negotiate (Liozu et al. 2011). However, the latest empirical work suggests the sales guys may be right. Recent studies suggest there is a positive link between delegation of pricing authority and business unit performance (Frenzen et al. 2010) and that delegating pricing authority can increase sales personnel motivation (Yuksel and Sutton-Brady 2011). My guess is that a delegation of control authority to the sales force raises their pricing confidence. Sales reps hate to be seen by the customer as having no authority, as this can greatly demotivate them and reduce their individual and collective self-esteem (Bohn 2001).

As you might guess, organizational design and the delegation of pricing authority are potentially explosive subjects. Get it right and you are in great shape. Get it wrong, and you can face rebellion—or worse. Unfortunately, behind door number one there may be sharks. And doors two, three, and four? More sharks. As we shall see in the following sections, all of the structures have drawbacks.

Centralized Versus Decentralized Pricing Options for Pricing Organizational Designs

To fill in the considerable blanks in the centralization literature, I decided to ask hundreds of managers with pricing responsibilities how their company handled pricing. Their answers suggested that leading from the center turns out to be an important factor in the success of a pricing system. The reasons for centralization's importance, however, are not what you may think. My research suggests that the success of center-led leadership is not due to their power to force the party line. What matters more is the platform that central leadership gives pricing specialists to diffuse pricing knowledge, to provide analytical support for pricing decisions, and to create intelligence and intellectual capital around the firm's pricing. In other words, center-led price management does not make enforcing prices easy, but centralized price leadership makes it easier to educate the organization about sophisticated pricing ideas, reducing the need for enforcement.

Organizations follow four kinds of price-management structures (Figure 4.1): decentralized, centralized, center-supported, and center-led (Liozu and Ecker 2012).

Decentralized Pricing

Decentralized pricing is the de facto organizational design for most companies when pricing is either managed badly or not managed at all.

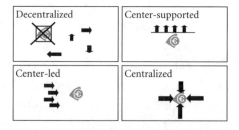

Figure 4.1 Types of price management structures

Headquarters hands down pricing guidelines but the actual prices are set in the field, at the discretion of on-the-ground sales reps. This system gives the sales force maximum flexibility, makes it possible to respond to local factors, and encourages the reps to take the initiative. The key measurement of success in this environment is revenue; in other words, as long as the customers are buying, the price is right.

These are the sources of its disadvantages as well. The structure gives management little control and transparency. There is a lack of direct ownership: when something goes wrong, no one is responsible for fixing it. As the success of the strategy is sales driven, it is also highly dependent on salespeople and their relationships with the clients. When a rep leaves a company, his knowledge of the customer and their price sensitivities is lost. But sometimes that is less of a problem than management believes; in a decentralized structure, the people considered the best salespeople are often only the best in terms of revenue, not profit. Lack of centralized control leads to inconsistency in pricing, revenue leakage, relationship-related discounting, and a loss of ability to set price levels.

Center-Supported Pricing

Center-supported pricing gives management a bit more control over actual prices. Companies that use it have recognized that they need more pricing discipline but have a sales function that is not prepared to yield any control or decision-making authority. The key measurement of success is process improvement, and the catalyst for those improvements is a department that is officially responsible for pricing and price setting. This pricing function supports the organization in a number of ways. It creates sales tools for evaluating the business, manages pricing systems, organizes price increases, ensures that list prices are printed, and enumerates pricing processes. Sometimes a company will invest in a specialized pricing system and place that under the responsibility of the pricing team. However, as impressive as this new dashboard may look, be careful when you put the vehicle in gear; this car probably lacks a brake and a steering wheel. The pricing team has no authority to influence profit margins. Instead, their role is limited to supporting the decisions and direction of the management.

The key advantage to center-supported pricing is that it gives the pricing leader some control over the price-entry process and establishes some basic pricing functionality. Everybody wins; center support leads to improved efficiencies and more process consistency, requires few new hires, and lets the sales force retain a lot of pricing flexibility.

Inevitably, the center-supported system has disadvantages. The biggest is that it does not lead; it simply supports. And that is a major difference. Center support only gives the company an illusion of pricing control. It will not have a significant impact on the bottom line. Center-supported companies still suffer from inconsistent offers and a tendency over time to settle on lowest-common-denominator prices. Revenue still tends to leak and the company still loses control. After a period of seeing no gains in profitability, companies that have tried center-supported pricing often revert to an entirely decentralized pricing structure.

Center-Led Pricing

Center-led pricing brings pricing expertise to a strategic level of the company, which then disseminates the knowledge and selected pricing responsibilities back to other parts of the organization through price bands, training, pricing processes, KPI reports that track average selling price, and price erosion. It provides analysis for new-product pricing opportunities, guidelines for making special offers to certain customers, input on list and target prices, and centralized trend monitoring. However, customer contracts remain local. The key measurements of success are profit and process improvement.

Center-led pricing offers a number of advantages. Standardizing offers streamlines and clarifies the ownership of particular processes, making it easier to implement any future changes. It adds more expertise to the price-setting process as well and improves consistency between local entities. Central monitoring also makes it easier to identify gray markets, to diffuse consistent knowledge, and to manage a pool of talent across the organization.

A center-led design improves pricing processes and takes functional ownership of pricing systems. It eventually creates a pricing intelligence community within the company. This brings information from many areas to a central point where trends, opportunities, and threats can be identified and evaluated and strategic options considered. By focusing on diffusing pricing knowledge and capabilities throughout the organization, center-led teams contribute to the building of organizational confidence and awareness of collective capability. They enable the company to better assess any competitors' moves in the market, such as determining whether a price change is a local phenomenon or a concerted action, and then select the appropriate response.

But there are, of course, trade-offs. The biggest is that although central pricing leaders have pricing responsibility, they lack pricing authority. Pricing leaders must persuade the affected business units to fall in line, but local decision makers can still override their advice. A certain amount of duplication in resources is inevitable as well, to ensure that central initiatives are implemented and local concerns addressed. Client offers may remain inconsistent in the end. Control is also indirect and achieved only by monitoring KPIs.

Creating a center-led system is also a lot of work. To successfully implement center-led pricing, the company must follow a change-management protocol to ensure that all company plans align with the company's pricing goals and that each unit makes decisions at the local level to support those goals. The pricing experts are responsible not only for tools and processes but also for establishing guidelines and skills development programs throughout the company. This is often a major adjustment for the company, particularly for sales. Center-led pricing brings more consistency and predictability to the business, but at the price of some of the sales force's flexibility, as they now must adhere to guidelines recommended by the experts and agreed to by leadership. They also need to pick up new skills to help them sell on value and understand the impact of their pricing offers on the company.

Pricing team members must also learn how to listen and how to persuade people despite their lack of authority. This is a stretch for many pricing experts who are never taught how to operate in matrix organizations. Conflicts and tensions often arise between field reps and the pricing team. Setting up a center-led management team demands special behavioral and psychological training, but most center-led companies don't make the investment. Not surprisingly, not many firms that take this approach succeed.

Centralized Pricing

Centralized pricing takes centralization one step further. A central team of experts and analysts is responsible for all pricing in the organization. In a large organization, a strongly centralized pricing function can ensure that the company gives its customers consistent prices and prevents price erosion. The pricing function is responsible for all processes, systems, and analysis and ultimately for the content of the offers made to clients. Focused on controlling prices and generally autocratic, centralized pricing managers measure profit and degree of compliance.

However, centralized pricing shares the disadvantages of most command-and-control systems. The response time and lack of flexibility will usually cost some sales. Reps may feel frustrated. Such centralized systems can also be culturally destructive. I recently visited a Fortune 500 industrial firm and met with all its pricing professionals. One division had implemented a centralized pricing design and controlled every pricing condition from headquarters. Prices had stabilized, but everything else was in flux. Account managers in this division told me about their discontent with the new design. Under the new system, they had lost their ability to have constructive and decisive discussions with customers. The sales force was losing credibility, stature, and prestige. Some customers had told their account managers point-blank that they had no reason to exist if they did not have the authority to negotiate directly with their clients. Others had done more than grumble about their lost autonomy; this division had already lost two sales stars who had decided they could not work in a nontrusting culture.

So no design is perfect. Some are better than others, but whether they are better will depend mostly on what circumstances you are facing, internal and external. That said, however, I do think that for the right company, center-led price management has some interesting possibilities.

Center-Led Management for Pricing: Design and Roles

I discovered the concept of center-led management as I reviewed the transcripts of my 2012 qualitative interviews. Unexpectedly, I found a sharp contrast in the organizational design between firms that deployed value-based pricing and those that used cost- or competition-based pricing. All firms using value-based pricing created specialized units composed of highly skilled professionals whose mission was to support the pricing decision-making process. These units ranged from a dedicated pricing team acting as internal consultants to a specialized market research team dedicated to voice of the customer projects (see Table 4.1). The names for this team varied, but each unit provided project-related support to managers who made pricing decisions specific to their section of the business.

My analysis of these results suggested to me that some of these firms had turned this pricing team into a center of analysis and pricing education rather than control. Five out of six sales and marketing respondents in firms using value-based pricing indicated that this central pricing function acted as a resource to improve managerial pricing management (see Table 4.2). By contrast, none of the six firms using cost-based pricing reported the existence of a similar pricing function.

To understand more about the significance of what my research had turned up, I explored literature for center-led management concepts and

Table 4.1 Evidence of role specialization in firms that use value-based pricing

---

"We have dedicated [functional] managers. They don't do anything else, and then just [customer research], and this is observation of the customer. It's videotaping of the customer. It's understanding what is the unarticulated needs of the customer, and of course, also the articulated needs."

"The way [Company] works is we have the business units in [Country] which are in charge of development. So they bring the products and then they bring overall pricing guidelines worldwide."

"You've got the senior manager of pricing, which is responsible for the pricing processes; continuous improvement for [the corporation] overall . . . and then within that group you have a few analysts who help manage the pricing within the system: one technical person, one person who helps on the reporting . . . one individual who helps out with projects like agreement review process [and] strategic business pricing. And we also have a group that focuses in on day-to-day maintenance of making sure price points in the system don't go below a certain threshold."

"In a development group . . . there's three people like [Name] who are development managers. We've got hundreds of development people in the world. . . . That's all they do. They don't sell a thing. . . . So they're doing the advanced design, advanced development."

"We have engineering services, our project managers . . . [who] can put together a cost justification analysis . . . The department is called Engineering Services . . . they'll bring in all the formulas/cost justifications from our customer's end."

"We have a pricing department. It's four people that are split by market segment, and they're responsible for doing quotes for new business or large—anything that's not under contract should come to them for pricing, to do a quote."

Table 4.2 Evidence of expertise centralization in firms that use value-based pricing

---

". . . we have three full-time equivalents for voice of the customer studies. We have that centrally. So whenever we develop a product for this market, we get them here and they set the whole system because it's a very formal thing."

"The overall team supports all of the [Company] North America . . . the profit desk underneath the pricing team can look to see whether or not the price points are too low."

"Pricing is actually at the corporate level here, it's marketing that has that pricing team underneath. So marketing is responsible for defining the price points."

"I am a corporate function, I go from business to business."

"When we wanna do something different and new, we hooked up with them [Central Team] [and] when we said, "You know, on our mature business, we got too many price points. We need to simplify this thing. How do you help us simplify?" . . . there's this group out there that knows [and] consults on this all the time. Why don't we tap into them, and let's start a project. [That] group is kinda looking for the best of the best in [Company] and in cross-training."

"We tap into our corporate sales and marketing [team] [and] say, "Hey, they've got professionals that know the terminology, the theory, and the strategy associated with pricing in general." And you do a little bit of negotiation role-playing and that sort of thing. So that's probably once a year or once every year and a half."

---

discovered a few practitioner papers on the topic in sourcing and supply chain management but almost no in-depth academic work. After further research of my own, I learned that center-led pricing had some important advantages for my respondents. Centralized pricing expertise and knowledge allows pricing and business professionals in other units to make better pricing decisions, to better implement technical pricing resources (systems, models, and tools), and to better manage their tactical pricing operations.

In this hybrid model (shown in Figure 4.2), compliance is gained through communication, coordination, conversation, and consensus, not decree. Internal pricing experts at the corporate level build a pricing-focused culture and deploy standardized approaches across all business

Figure 4.2 Centralized versus decentralized pricing

entities to capture synergies and leverage best practices. They develop a toolbox of pricing methods, processes, systems, and concepts that business leaders and tactical pricing experts can select from and operationalize in their divisions or business entities. They don't tell. They persuade.

One executive described the company structure this way:

> You've got the senior manager of pricing, which is responsible for the pricing processes; continuous improvement for [the corporation] overall . . . and then within that group you have a few analysts who help manage the pricing within the system: one technical person, one person who helps on the reporting . . . one individual who helps out with projects like agreement review process [and] strategic business pricing. And we also have a group that focuses in on day-to-day maintenance of making sure price points in the system don't go below a certain threshold.

Unlike a center-controlled model, the pricing team and the field operational teams at this company had a high level of mutual respect. They worked hand in hand and had strongly aligned goals. The divisional sales force relied on the pricing team for support, guidance, and coaching. Their relationship was not confrontational or adversarial, as it can be in many organizations where pricing is not well managed. The pricing team saw itself as a partner to the marketing, innovation, and sales teams.

Many companies are convinced. A number of best-in-class firms have adopted this organizational design for pricing, including DuPont, DSM, 3M, Schneider Electric, and Eastman Chemicals. They call them pricing centers of excellence. In these firms, the roles and activities of specialized pricing experts strongly and positively encourage the adoption of pricing activities and programs because they can design and communicate a corporate pricing vision in a way that convinces everyone that it is in her best interest to comply. In these organizations, the credibility of pricing and value excellence teams is incredibly high and their presence is felt everywhere. They act as internal consultants who troubleshoot divisional pricing problems, their authority enhanced by strong support from top management.

The disadvantage of center-led pricing is that it's harder. Center-led pricing can't work without top management support. This organizational design also does not guarantee that value-based pricing will follow automatically. In fact, some center-led pricing teams focus on optimizing cost-based or competition-based pricing systems. Nor is center-led the right structure for every firm. Other top firms have centralized pricing and removed all authority from their business units, and succeeded with that as well. The key is to design a structure—and prepare to keep redesigning the structure—based on customer needs, market dynamics, and changes in the internal organizational culture. That said, I have yet to meet a firm with a high level of pricing maturity that uses a totally decentralized pricing architecture.

In a center-led pricing organization, specialized pricing teams serve eight basic functions (Figure 4.3):

Internal consulting. Pricing teams operate as an internal consulting firm, charging divisions for their services and expertise. In these organizations, business units are considered clients and project requests are prioritized based on the return on investment to both the division and the corporation.

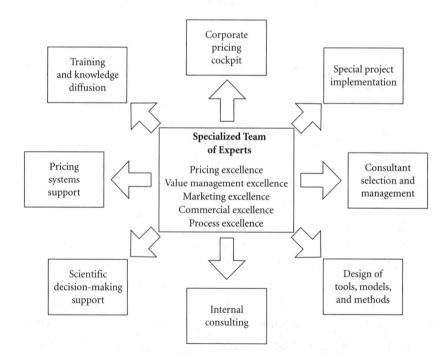

Figure 4.3 The role of center-led teams

Scientific decision-making support. The internal pricing team becomes a center for research and analysis. The team provides a set of analytics and pricing research in a toolbox format. Business units then decide if they want to run, for example, a segmentation analysis or conduct conjoint research, and use the pricing team as an internal resource. This leads to cost savings, an easier scaling-up process, and consistent analysis.

Pricing systems support. When organizations decide to implement a price analytics solution, they usually consider various options and, in the most efficient companies, deploy one solution across multiple business units. Pricing teams serve as pricing IT support and process experts for the software implementations and help divisions with blueprint analysis, process simplification, and deployment. In organizations running more sophisticated pricing software, the team may even include several IT professionals.

Training and knowledge diffusion. This is probably the most common role of the pricing team. Pricing experts craft and deploy basic, intermediate, and advanced training modules. They maintain a flow of pricing knowledge circulating across the business units and share not only prices but concepts and best practices regarding strategic channel management, value-based selling, negotiation, and so on. They work with product-management teams to deliver powerful product and business model training.

Corporate pricing cockpit. Pricing experts rely more and more on dashboards to see the impact of the pricing transformation on corporate and divisional results. As part of the pricing council, the pricing team must track and measure corporate and divisional key performance indicators and assemble them in an intuitive display. The metrics tracked on this dashboard or cockpit have a secondary value too; they serve to remind top executives of the ROI of the pricing transformation and the value created by the pricing team.

Special project implementation. The pricing team may also be tapped for special projects related to the pricing transformation. Every division is different in the challenges it faces, and occasionally systems must be custom-built to support special needs or challenges.

Consultant selection and management. Pricing teams also sometimes assist in writing up requests for pricing proposals and screening consulting offers. Their work serves two critical purposes: first, to clarify the company's true needs, and second, to compare consulting offers through an apples-to-apples lens.

Design of tools, models, and methods. Finally, pricing teams in a center-led design build proprietary tools and models for divisions as they are needed. Such tools include dollarization models for value measurement, total cost of ownership tools, value-in-use models, advanced cost modeling, and databases to track competitive information. Well executed, such teams can provide a sustainable advantage that cannot be copied by competitors.

The center-led pricing management architecture is widely recognized as the best design for pricing management. However, just because it's the best does not mean it's the right design for everyone, any more than a Porsche engine is right for every car. In fact, when facing strong internal change resistance, center-led pricing teams can quickly lose their power. As mentioned earlier in the chapter, center-led teams rely on the business units they advise to embrace their recommendations and follow their guidelines. They also usually need the top leaders to encourage their cooperation. If those factors are absent and business unit leaders continue to pursue their own pricing agenda, forming a pricing council within a division may be a better way to ease the change process and encourage the adoption of pricing guidelines. This is why a center-led pricing management design is often complemented with a pricing council.

Design Your Pricing Council to Become a Strategic Weapon

One key to successful center-led pricing is the pricing council, a deliberative group that focuses specifically on pricing issues. The idea of a pricing council is becoming more and more popular among pricing professionals, but I think most organizations have undersold their value. I have seen pricing councils and pricing processes designed in a way that is so unique and invisible from the outside that it cannot be imitated by the competition. With some modifications in design, I believe a pricing council can become a strategic competitive weapon for the organization.

How you frame it, who sits in it, how frequently it meets, how long it meets for, where it meets, what the agenda looks like, and how council actions are communicated are all questions that should be integrated in the overall design. Thoughtfully organized, a highly functioning council will generally drive better pricing decisions, better long-term performance, and sometimes even a competitive advantage.

Based on what I found in my research and in my own practical experience, the success of a pricing council depends on taking some fairly common-sense measures:

- Have the CEO, a C-suite executive, or another top leader sit in on every pricing council meeting. This is the best way to elevate the conversation, to get people to participate, and to get quick decisions made.

- Make sure the team includes sales, marketing, pricing, finance, innovation, management, R&D, operations, and maybe even HR. The more the merrier.

- Set a consistent agenda. For example, you might send the latest results of the pricing dashboard in advance of every meeting so that the first 20 to 30 minutes of the meeting can be spent discussing specific questions, outliers, and special cases, not simply reviewing results. Make sure you leave time for discussions of new-product pricing and other strategic subjects.

- Schedule meetings to be short. It is better to have one 60-minute meeting every two weeks than a two-hour meeting once a month. People will lose focus and interest. This is also why the dashboard results should be reviewed by participants before the meeting. The last thing you want is to spend 60 minutes going over each key performance indicator.

- Make sure you have a balance of topics, so you never neglect a key area of concern.

The basics of running a pricing council are not rocket science. What becomes a bit trickier is to design a pricing council that is capable of sponsoring a new pricing system. Well designed and well run, such a forum can break down organizational silos, disrupt mechanical pricing routines, and become more creative in nature. When not properly designed, a pricing council meeting becomes just another pricing meeting.

As with so much in pricing, a lot of the success of the pricing council depends on the leader; for example, how well the leader is able to make the council:

A platform for candid and open discussions

Pricing is a subject that generates tensions and conflicts. Having open and candid discussions in a safe and nonjudgmental environment can help create greater alignment in pricing tactics. The council can be the platform to address tough issues, potential tensions, and organizational breakdowns—but only if the leader can set the right tone and make sure that people have a chance to vent, share, and give constructive feedback.

A platform for continuous improvement in value and pricing management

Value and pricing management can be complex. Creating a culture of mindfulness in the pricing council, making it a place where problems can be discussed openly and solved together, is important. The council moderator should seek continuous improvement in pricing and not point fingers at anyone for bad decisions or a difficult pricing environment.

A platform to create a higher level of rationality

When teams openly and mindfully discuss new-product pricing and when they have access to scientific data supporting the pricing levels, they encourage a greater sense of rationality. To help promote a rational, dispassionate discussion, leaders should encourage sharing the science behind pricing decisions.

A platform for strategic conversation

The council leader should try to make sure that most of the meeting is spent reviewing, discussing, and challenging the overall pricing strategy. Pay special attention to strategic project review, new-product pricing, value creation and capture activities, and competitive market dynamics. Keep trying to look at the big picture: Are we living our pricing vision? Are we getting our money's worth on our pricing investments? Are we as differentiated as we imagine? If not, should we revise our market strategy?

A platform for creativity and dynamic change

Finally, the pricing council should be a place of creative exploration and experimentation. The leader should encourage proposals to further the overall pricing strategy and to keep pricing aligned with the evolving marketing strategy. We live in a dynamic and competitive global business world. Value and pricing strategies and tactics cannot be static. Pricing strategies have to respond rapidly to changes in the market or you can dig yourself into a worse position than if you were still running a cost-plus system.

Competing by Design: Unique Design for Competitive Advantage

Sometimes, pricing systems can be designed in unique ways that represent a competitive weapon that cannot be easily imitated (Dutta et al. 2002; Dierickx and Cool 1989). Often, such unique designs look off-kilter and seem to have been put together in ways that really should not work. Their designs do not fit well in the conventional management structure theories, and on paper they look ineffective, overlapping, and wasteful. But organizational architecture isn't physics—or if it is like physics, it's more like quantum mechanics, where the ordinary rules don't always apply. The CEOs of these organizations clearly approached pricing design with intention and had a strong desire to be differentiated, and in the end, they achieved it, even if they went about it in a way that from the outside looks completely convoluted.

I would like to be able to offer a single best design for a pricing system, but my research suggests that no system is inherently better. Each design offers advantages and disadvantages that executives will need to weigh in the context of their own situation. To add further to the complexity, the right answer may change over time and will depend on the firm's pricing maturity and the competition it faces in the market. Sometimes, the best solution is to start with one design and then adopt another when more mature pricing skills and processes are in place.

In the end, leaders must first establish their pricing goals and strategies and then determine the kind of architecture they will need to achieve the increase in pricing power that they want. They will have to consider trade-offs between various variables related to pricing: delegation, speed of response to customers and the sales force, approach to price decisions, and more. A company facing tough competition may choose a decentralized structure that gives the sales force flexibility and leads to fast response times for customer offers. On the other hand, a company worried about internal costs may choose a center-supported strategy. When the objective is price consistency, contract compliance, KPI stability, superior pricing, analysis, and control over gray markets, a centralized strategy may be the right choice.

The company's culture and capabilities will make a difference as well. For a company with serious deficiencies in its pricing skill capabilities, centralization would probably be a mistake. Similarly, if the pricing func-

About the Research

My findings strongly suggest that the role of executives in the corporate suite is essential for the design and adoption of pricing technologies and resources in firms. But they can achieve only so much on their own. A unique organizational architecture for the promotion of a culture of change and pricing knowledge diffusion should be a top priority for many senior managers. The bulk of my research supports the proposition that a unique organizational design for the pricing function (emphasizing champions, change capacity, center-led pricing, capabilities, and confidence) leads firms to greater relative firm performance.

Finally, although one size does not fit all, my research suggests that a center-led design for pricing management does seem to contribute positively to the development of technical pricing capabilities, as center-led pricing management combines the strength of a centralized and a decentralized structure (Figure 4.2).

tion does not have a strong team in place yet, centralization is probably a bad idea.

Conclusion: A Dynamic Design

One thing I have learned as a management scholar and as a manager is that any collision between theory and practice tends not to end well for the theory. Individuals act in unexpected ways and so do organizations. However, unpredictability doesn't mean that there aren't instructive patterns. A strong pricing council tends to be a good thing, as does thoughtful pricing council leadership. Although I would not say that there is only one way to run a pricing process—companies must find a model that suits their culture—the companies I have reviewed that have sophisticated pricing programs all follow some variant of a center-led process. For some, center-led pricing doesn't work very well, but it often seems to work better than the other two extremes. To paraphrase Churchill's line about democracy, center-led pricing is the worst pricing organizational structure in the world—except for all the others.

The centralization of pricing expertise and knowledge allows pricing and business professionals in decentralized structures to make better pricing decisions, to better implement technical pricing resources (systems, models, and tools), and to manage their tactical pricing operations. In this hybrid model, compliance is gained through communication, coordination, conversation, and consensus. Firms that adopt center-led teams often call them pricing excellence teams, marketing excellence teams, or simply internal consulting teams. The roles and activities of such groups of specialized experts, as shown in Figure 4.3, can strongly and positively impact the adoption of the change agenda as long as pricing champions design and communicate a corporate pricing vision to which both centralized and decentralized teams can adhere.

Center-Led Price Management: Some Tips to Get Started

1. Analyze the culture of your organization and understand the power players by individual and department.

2. Benchmark your organizational structure for other departments such as R&D, sourcing, and the supply chain to understand how they are structured and how they evolved through time.

3. Focus on making the pricing council the central forum for price management and collaboration.

4. Remember that "structure follows strategy." Once the overall pricing strategy is set, focus on designing the best pricing structure to match the vision and goals of the overall strategy.

5. Before you recommend a pricing structure, factor in your organization's level of pricing maturity, its culture, the complexity of its pricing problems, and the readiness of the current pricing team.

5 Capabilities
Social and Technical Assets and Activities

In a learning organization, leaders are designers, stewards, and teachers. They are responsible for building organizations where people continually expand their capabilities to understand complexity, clarify vision, and improve mental models—that is, they are responsible for learning.
Peter Senge, *The Art and Practice of the Learning Organization*

The next *C* of the 5C model stands for capabilities. Pricing capabilities are the tools, skills, and processes that companies use to set their prices—everything from the software to the skills of the price-setting team—and they're the foundation of the transformational model shown in Chapter 2 of the book. In fact, at every stage of the transformation, technical and non-technical pricing capabilities are deployed in the organization. In Stage 5 of the model, large-scale enterprise solutions are introduced on top of the strong pricing culture developed early in the journey. This is why capabilities are treated in third position after champions and center-led management. After the CEO is involved in the pricing road map and the center-led model is deployed across the organization, then pricing resources and activities can be executed stage by stage. Many times, pricing software or pricing tools are deployed without proper buy-in from the organization and without proper scoping of the overall project. That is a fatal error made by pricing professionals and their sponsors.

Executives new to strategic pricing often tend to make two serious planning errors. The first error is believing that you'll need to give only your marketing and salespeople training on the new system. In fact, nearly everyone in the organization needs some degree of understanding about these tools and skills. This is why I call the pricing transformation an organizational transformation. In my experience, pricing capability-building programs should include everyone involved in customer interactions—and that includes people from the front line and people in the C-suite. The second is thinking that advanced pricing capabilities are just something you buy—that all you need to do is invest in a new software module and you'll be good to go. In fact, as we'll see in the next section, there are many different kinds of capabilities, and unfortunately, the most important can't simply be installed.

What the Literature Is Telling Us

Resource-based view of the firm. I anchor my definition of a business capability on the work of earlier scholars who saw the firm as a collection of resources or capabilities. Barney (1991) considered the firm to be a framework in which resources or assets are combined to create competitive advantage and superior performance. Other scholars criticized this resource-based view of the firm because it failed to explain how firms obtained, developed, and deployed those resources in the first place (Morgan, Vorhies, and Mason 2009; Priem and Butler 2001). Since then, scholars have filled the theory out by focusing on the activities and processes necessary to develop and leverage tangible and intangible resources. They have defined capabilities as a special type of resource whose purpose is to improve the productivity of the company's other assets.

Capabilities and competitive advantage. As the foregoing list suggests, success is not just about what technical resources are deployed but how they are used—the special configuration of skills that enable the company to offer something its competitors can't, or as Day puts it, the "complex bundles of skills and accumulated knowledge, exercised through organizational processes, that enable firms to coordinate activities and make use of their assets" (Day 1994:38). Capabilities are the glue that joins assets so that they can be deployed advantageously. Such capabilities may be obvious, hidden, or embedded in the fabric of the organization (Makadok 2001; Teece, Pisano, and Shuen 1997), distributed among various individuals, or dispersed (Leonard-Barton 1992).

Pricing capabilities refer, on the one hand, to the price-setting capability within a firm (identifying competitor prices, setting pricing strategy, translating from pricing strategy to price), and, on the other, to the price-getting capability (convincing customers of price-change logic or negotiating price changes with major accounts).

What Are Pricing Capabilities?

The distinction between resources and capabilities can be a little difficult to make, particularly in a world with so many intangible assets, but it comes down to know-how: if the firm is a bottle of Coca-Cola, the resources are the plastic for the bottle, carbonated water, and fructose; capabilities are the method of manufacturing and the marketing that turn those ingredients into *the real thing*.

Dutta, Zbaracki, and Bergen (2003) described pricing capabilities as the ability to translate a pricing strategy into price, to convince the customer on the price change logic, to negotiate price changes within major customers, to develop internal pricing management, or to capture value through price. Other scholars have considered pricing capabilities mostly as part of a larger set of marketing capabilities, including product development, channel management, market communication, selling, market information management, marketing planning, and marketing implementation (Vorhies and Morgan 2005).

The resources and capabilities needed for advanced pricing span an unusually wide range of dimensions (Figure 5.1). The capabilities include

Pricing Dimensions	Examples of Resources	Examples of Activities
Infrastructure	Hardware, communication tools	Select appropriate technology, deploy and conduct user training.
Analytics	Dashboards, advanced analytics	Conduct analysis: waterfall, pricing cloud, price elasticity, pricing sensitivity, cost-to-serve, etc.
Information systems	ERP, optimization, VBP software	Select appropriate technology, implement pricing module, and manage pricing operations.
Tools and models	TCO, value-in-use, cost models	Design proprietary tools and models to perform and manage output for TCO analysis.
Advanced methods	Segmentation, pricing research, VOC	Conduct conjoint and willingness-to-pay research.

Figure 5.1 Technical pricing capabilities

specific pricing activities that need to be performed by pricing, finance, and IT professionals. Buying and selling is still an intensely human activity, and even the most advanced pricing technologies require people to run the software and apply the insights that its reports yield. Not surprisingly, this breadth of possibilities has made it difficult for practitioners to decide exactly which capabilities they should develop.

They also can't be added in an ad hoc way. To be effective, these systems must be rolled out in a particular order.

The first set to get right is the IT infrastructure. Pricing initiatives frequently go wrong when a finance or IT team is persuaded to install a vendor's idea of what a pricing system should look like without considering their own needs. In fact, bolting a generic pricing module to your ERP system can be counterproductive, adding complexity without solving the problem. Companies often run similar risks with pricing optimization software. As with any kind of powerful tool, it can help you as well as hurt you, depending on how you use it. This infrastructure should include the power to:

- *Perform basic analytics.* The system should generate reports and data dashboards, spot price erosion, price sensitivity analysis, and cost-to-serve analysis. A segmentation study is generally quite useful as well.

- *Research prices.* Only 15 percent of firms do systematic primary pricing research. This means that in many industries, a willingness to invest in research and advanced analytics such as conjoint analysis can create an important advantage. However, don't forget that part of that investment needs to be in hiring professionals who are able to interpret this newfound wealth of information. Managers should ask themselves: Do we have the technical talent we need to manage all this new data? Will we need to write a program to interpret the results? Who will teach sales and marketing how to read these new reports?

- *Carry a thick wallet.* A value-based pricing program can be expensive to execute, six figures or more for one or two products when proper segmentation is conducted, voice-of-customer research performed, and the value drivers properly quantified. The investment can quickly reach the million-dollar zone when value-based pricing is deployed at a larger scale. The good news is that if such assets are properly installed and used, pricing practitioners tell me that they typically get back $7–$10 on every dollar they invest.

If choosing the right capabilities is an essential part of a successful pricing transformation, picking the wrong ones is the first step toward failure. As pricing pioneer Shantanu Dutta put it in a 2002 article, "If pricing isn't a strategic capability—a contributor to a company's ability to implement its strategy—it's probably a strategic liability" (Dutta et al. 2002). Sometimes weak capabilities can lead not just to underperformance, but destruction. As far back as 60 years ago, Backman (1953) observed, "the graveyard of business is filled with the skeletons of companies that attempted to base their prices solely on costs." In our own time, we have seen pricing myopia kill many companies, especially in industries where disruptive competitors are undermining traditional pricing models or sales channels. Polaroid, for instance, was so wedded to its old razor blade approach—underpricing its cameras and making money on instant film—that the company collapsed when digital photography took off. Although Polaroid had a strong tradition of innovation and the technical know-how to be an early entrant to digital photography and instant photographic printing, its lack of flexibility in its pricing model led it straight into bankruptcy (Dutta et al. 2002).

In theory, a company might also hurt itself by overinvesting in pricing capabilities, but in practice I have found that they almost never do. In my survey, I found that every company I contacted that had added value-based pricing capabilities—including small and medium-sized companies and those operating in commodity industries or in Asia (which has a reputation for tough pricing)—had benefited from the investment. Other studies have also shown that pricing capabilities correlate positively to firm performance (Berggren and Eek 2007; Dutta et al. 2002; Hallberg 2008). My survey results suggest that no matter what kind of company you have or what state your industry is in, you can profit from cultivating tangible and intangible pricing capabilities.

What are these capabilities, exactly? Most pricing experts allude to them vaguely, but I think they can be detailed in specific terms. For my part, I think the best way to define pricing capabilities is to think of the knowledge, skills, and organizational structures that support the four core activities of pricing.

The first activity, *identifying competitor prices*, demands technical know-how about competitive products in the pricing team and sales force knowledge of field sources that have reliable competitive price information. Cross-functional teams need competitive product information, and the sales force needs to be able to work with select customers to establish competitive prices. Together, the team must be able to define functionally equivalent products, track competitive prices (such as offering a special discount for the purposes of price discovery), and assess competitive price information.

The second activity, *setting and executing the pricing strategy*, requires system development expertise, pricing strategy expertise, database skills, financial analysis skills, customer price sensitivity, and the ability to build scenarios of the customer response to a given action. Knowledge of differing assumptions and the ability to reach consensus on assumptions about customers, to coordinate knowledge of different pricing strategies around the enterprise, and to disseminate information on pricing actions to different channels are all essential. The team needs to be able to collect customer purchase histories, track past pricing actions and analyze their impact, and resolve conflicts.

The third activity, *convincing customers of the logic behind the pricing change*, demands the mastery of a pricing tool kit and a deep understanding of price change effects. It also takes a deep understanding of the customer and an ability to separate genuine concerns from negotiating postures. This requires developing an understanding of different perspectives; building a consensus within the firm, including the sales force, about the new prices; and decoding the customer response. The team needs to be able to exchange information with customers' own pricing systems, identify the effect on customers' customers, and maintain a steady flow of information from sales to the pricing team. Perhaps most importantly, they need to be able to prepare a presentation explaining and justifying every single pricing change.

The fourth activity, *negotiating price changes with major customers*, demands a deep knowledge of the firm's customer relationships, know-how about competitive offerings, an understanding of customer negotiating strategy, cross-functional negotiating expertise, and an ability to conduct customer price sensitivity analysis. This entails creating a consensus within the pricing team about the new prices, within the negotiating team about the negotiation strategy, and within the C-suite about the overall strategy. Once the prices are negotiated, customer assessments will need to be gathered and negotiating materials developed.

Not every capability is created equal. Some theorists have argued that the capabilities that matter most are dynamic, "the firm's ability to integrate, build and reconfigure internal and external competences to address rapidly changing environments" (Teece, Pisano, and Shuen 1997:516). To be truly distinctive (Day 1994) and inimitable (Dierickx and Cool 1989), companies need capabilities that reflect the "interconnectedness between individual capabilities, business processes, competitive strategy and firm environment" (Hallberg 2008:33). These dynamic capabilities also need to reflect the organization's ability to achieve innovative forms of competitive advantage (Leonard-Barton 1992). Considering Coke again, a dynamic capability may mean not just the ability to produce an iconic soft drink in one country or even a bunch of countries, but to develop beverages that will appeal to people who don't like fizzy water at all. In pricing, this means thinking beyond supporting a particular software system toward a consistently value-oriented approach that will continue to add insights despite advances in technology, an evolution of the competitive landscape, and the ups and downs of the investment cycle.

By definition, such dynamic capabilities will be largely intangible, but unfortunately, scholars haven't yet agreed on how to separate intangible from tangible capabilities, let alone what they might be. Nadler and Tushman even define a firm's capabilities as a system that can't be fully captured on a piece of paper (1990)!

In pricing, however, we can be somewhat more specific. I have found, in analyzing 44 interviews with executives about pricing, that the executives often draw a distinction between formal technical capabilities and informal organizational capabilities. Formal technical capabilities are assets that involve software, key performance indicators, and other more quantitative capabilities. Informal organizational capabilities are the sorts of things

Visa might call "priceless"—beliefs, positive communication, and group morale.

The survey results suggested that formal and technical capabilities made it possible to make better pricing decisions, while informal and organizational capabilities enabled them to take advantage of those new insights (Figure 5.2). The distinction between the two types of capabilities is essential to understand the main argument of this book. Formal capabilities can be copied. Should your company decide to deploy a pricing optimization software solution, your competitors will quickly find out what you use and decide either to buy a copy for themselves or to deploy a competing platform. Informal capabilities can't be copied; these capabilities are a matter of culture, organizational design, and leadership style. They are intangible in nature and, as such, cannot be easily imitated. This is why so many companies end up disappointed with their pricing investments. Buying the same frying pan as Emeril won't make you Emeril.

This conclusion about the importance of intangible capabilities may seem counterintuitive given the tremendous advances in pricing technology in recent years, but reflect a bit and you'll see that it makes sense. The more advanced the pricing technology deployed by the organization, the

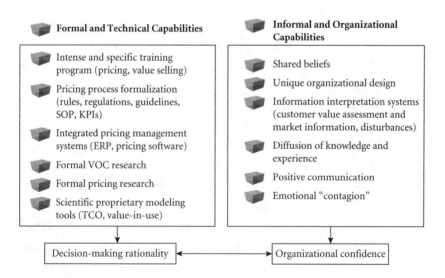

Figure 5.2 Pricing capabilities derived through qualitative inquiry

greater the complexity, because users and teams now need to create systems that integrate the technology into their practice. The deployment of advanced pricing technology also demands greater team interaction in pricing activities, greater organizational adaptation, and a potential redesign of roles and job descriptions. Often, new sets of skills must be learned in order to handle the software. The rising level of complexity demands new kinds of management as well, because it can't be led very well by old-style command-and-control bosses (Liozu and Hinterhuber 2012b). Instead, teams involved in the pricing journey work autonomously with little top-down control and intervention to ensure that the transformation stays on track. In other words, my research suggests that a pricing transformation takes more than revolutionary technology. It takes a revolution.

As with any revolution, the odds against success are fairly high. Success requires careful luck and some careful planning. Fortunately, there is some good data about which capabilities tend to matter most.

Pricing Capabilities and Firm Performance

A number of studies have found that pricing capabilities correlate with firm performance (Berggren and Eek 2007; Dutta et al. 2003; Hallberg 2008). Developing pricing capabilities significantly and positively influences firm performance, including sales, pricing, and profit. The executives I interviewed early in my research journey all agreed that acquiring tools, methods, and software greatly improved their ability to define pricing levels. But which capabilities matter most? In my subsequent surveys, most pricing executives agreed that price-setting capabilities, price-negotiation capabilities, value- and price-communication capabilities, and pricing processes and systems are all extremely good investments.

Over the past four years, three academic surveys with over 1,812 pricing and business practitioners showed a positive and significant relationship between pricing capabilities and relative firm performance (Liozu and Hinterhuber 2013). Built on work by other behavioral scientists and pricing experts, twelve critical technical pricing capabilities were identified and operationalized in multiple surveys. The result is unequivocal. The more you invest in these twelve capabilities, the better your performance in pricing,

---

About the Research

My conclusions rest on three separate empirical studies conducted in 2011 with support from three professional organizations: the Professional Pricing Society, the Young
Presidents' Organization, and the Strategic Account Management Association. I chose
these organizations based on their global representativeness in their respective fields,
their extended network, the quality of the membership base, and their overall reputation with practitioners. All three organizations supported the research inquiries by
launching multiple email communications to their members and by assisting with the
measurement of communication statistics. All three demonstrated exemplary commitment to academic research and to bridging theory and practice in the field of pricing.

The three studies were conducted from March through July 2011 and included a
total of 1,812 complete responses on a common set of constructs.

Pricing Capabilities Scale. Since there was little empirical precedent for measuring pricing capabilities, we developed a multiple-item scale in accordance with an
operational definition (Kerlinger and Lee 1999) by relying on our qualitative work and
on extant literature. I used twelve items ranging from 1 (*much worse than competitors*)

---

profit, and sales compared to your competitors. Furthermore, when I tested
the 5C model statistically in 2014 (Liozu, Hinterhuber, and Somers 2014),
pricing capabilities turned out to be the *C* that contributed most to firm
performance.

Besides these technical and powerful pricing capabilities, social capabilities are also critical (Dutta et al. 2002). Dutta and other researchers have
found over and over again not only that pricing capabilities relate to company performance, but also that the intangible (social capital) aspects of
pricing capabilities are at least as important as the tangible. In 2002, Dutta
and colleagues (2002) argued that the combination of capabilities related
to systems, human, and social dimensions of pricing as shown in Figure 5.3
constituted superior intellectual and organizational capital that could yield
a competitive advantage.

Adopting technical capabilities may not be as easy as it sounds, but the
process is at least easy to understand. As we'll see in the next section, adding
human and social capabilities is much trickier.

to 7 (*much better than competitors*) to operationalize this scale. The twelve items were as follows:

Using pricing skills and systems to respond quickly to market changes

Knowledge of competitors' pricing tactics

Doing an effective job of pricing products/services

Monitoring competitors' prices and price changes

Sticking to the price list and minimizing discounts

Quantifying customers' willingness to pay

Measuring and quantifying differential economic value versus competition

Measuring and estimating price elasticity for products/services

Designing proprietary tools to support pricing decisions

Conducting value-in-use analysis or total cost of ownership

Designing and conducting specific pricing training programs

Developing a proprietary internal price-management process

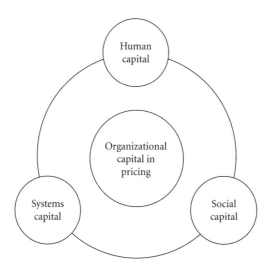

Figure 5.3 Organizational capital in pricing

Getting Social Capabilities Right

Scholars have long noted the importance of such social and organizational factors in the success or failure of information systems development (Luna-Reyes et al. 2005). Information systems experts are almost unanimous in linking many IT failures to an inability to manage the organizational impact of IT investments (Doherty and King 2005). Yet the development of better techniques to manage technological systems changes has been incredibly slow. As far back as 1964, one scholar (Leavitt) proposed a sociotechnical model to better understand the interactions between technology and the organization. Leavitt proposed that any given sociotechnical system needed to incorporate four basic elements: building system activities (development tools and the technical platform), actors (users, managers, and designers), tasks (goals and deliverables), and structure (project organization and in-stitutional arrangements). He warned that a working system needed strong interactions between the four elements of the model as well as the ability to adapt in order to keep the "system state" stable.

Unfortunately, this is easier said than done. Fifty years later, IT failures remain common, and pricing technology is no exception. I have seen many companies implement a multimillion-dollar pricing system only to find that no one will use it. Problems outside the company can affect it too: a disruption in the economy or the emergence of radical technology in the market may lead to a need for the system to be reconfigured and realigned (Lyytinen and Newman 2008).

A Sociotechnical Perspective on Pricing

This suggests that managers leading a pricing transformation must think not only about their software and hardware, but about how the organization will interact with the system. One way to structure this process is to work from Albert Cherns's sociotechnical design principles. Cherns (1976), then an associate of the Tavistock Institute, a British social science think tank, developed nine sociotechnical design principles, listed in Table 5.1, to help planners better integrate systems with their users' capacities and needs.

Cherns argued that every system should be considered from nine van-tage points:

Table 5.1 Sociotechnical design principles

Principle 1	Compatibility
Principle 2	Minimal critical specifications
Principle 3	Sociotechnical criterion
Principle 4	Multifunctionality principle
Principle 5	Boundary location
Principle 6	Information sharing
Principle 7	Support congruence
Principle 8	Human-centered design
Principle 9	Incompletion

- *Compatibility.* The process of design must be compatible with the objective of the transformation.
- *Minimal critical specifications.* The specifications of the transformation must be somewhat adaptable to incorporate change.
- *The sociotechnical criterion.* Work processes must be designed using the experience of all and with the user in mind.
- *The multifunctionality principle.* The system must be adaptable and able to evolve based on the usage of every function and hierarchical level.
- *Boundary location.* The boundaries of the transformation facilitate knowledge sharing and change capacity.
- *Information sharing.* Information must flow freely and not be blocked by bureaucracy.
- *Support congruence.* Support systems among team members involved in the transformation promote cooperation and build collective confidence.
- *Human-centered design.* Human values should be at the center of the transformation.
- *Incompletion.* The journey never ends, because design excellence requires perseverance, adaptation to changing dynamics, and many iterative processes.

Most of these principles can be adopted for the design of a transformational journey over multiple years that involves the development of many pricing capabilities. In particular, information must flow freely and not be blocked by bureaucracy; support systems among team members involved in the transformation must promote cooperation and build collective confidence; human values must be at the center of the transformation; and, finally, the organization needs to be prepared for an endless journey, because pricing excellence requires perseverance, adaptation to changing dynamics, and many iterative processes. Sociotechnical design theorists argue that the role of people in a technical system should never be of secondary importance: "although technology and organizational structures may change, the rights and needs of the employee must be given as high a priority as those of the non-human parts of the system" (Mumford 2006).

Pricing Capabilities Require Both Experiential and Transformative Learning

A key aspect of advanced pricing capabilities is the collective knowledge of the pricing team. Companies develop pricing knowledge and capabilities over time (Dutta et al. 2003); how quickly depends on the ability of the actors to learn the material (Cohen and Levinthal 1990; Zahra and George 2002; Szulanski 1996). Their acquisition of prior knowledge not only provides a base but makes it easier to learn new material, "to recognize the value of new information, assimilate it, and apply it to commercial ends" (Cohen and Levinthal 1990).

Experimentation is an important requirement for the internalization of pricing concepts, frames of reference, language, and forms of interaction. Experimentation "fuels the discovery and creation of knowledge and thereby leads to the development and improvement of products, processes, systems and organizations" (Thomke 2003:1). Experiments yield information that comes from understanding what works and does not work—and the misses may be more important than the hits. But the most important advantage of experiential learning through experiments is that it provides a valid way for managers to observe and interpret past experiences (Green and Taber 1978).

Experiential learning alone won't assure a successful transformation to pricing excellence, however. My own research suggests that in firms using cost-based or competition-based pricing, preexisting frames of reference are powerful in guiding pricing decisions. Habits of mind, routines, and legacy practices and mentality or mind-sets (Mezirow 2000) are deeply ingrained in the firm's culture and can be overcome only through transformation of these frames or references, routines, norms, and schemas to make them more inclusive, open, and "emotionally capable of change" (Mezirow 2000). However, in combination with transformative learning (building on prior knowledge to "construe a new or revised interpretation of the meaning of one's experience in order to guide future action" [Mezirow 1996, 2000]), the organization can develop new frames of reference.

Conclusion: The Limits of Capabilities

It's easy to deploy pricing software. The challenge is to get people to use it and use it again, so often that it becomes part of them. Over the past four years, I have spoken with many executives and pricing professionals puzzled by the lack of adoption of their systems, their models and tools, and most of all the scientific approach to pricing they are trying to inculcate. Somehow, they had expected that people would just sort of see the usefulness of smarter pricing and start doing things the new way. I have even met several companies that deployed advanced pricing optimization software without any sort of discussion with the people who would use the system. These may seem like obvious mistakes, but they still happen all the time.

In the end, a capability is just a possibility. The next challenge is to fulfill the potential those capabilities represent. To achieve assimilation and internalization of pricing resources and assets, the organization needs four more Cs: champions, center-led management, change-management skills, and confidence. Only with all five of these organizational and social capabilities in place can the firm integrate and internalize pricing resources and assets in the social fabric and culture of the organization.

Capabilities: Some Tips to Get Started

1. Conduct a pricing capabilities assessment (PCA) to evaluate the general pricing knowledge in your teams.

2.   As part of your PCA, conduct a pricing infrastructure audit to list all relevant methods, tools, systems, and other assets being used today to manage pricing operations.

3.   Conduct personal interviews as part of the PCA to identify the capacity of the organization to absorb new processes, new systems, and new tools. Evaluate the organization's capacity to change and learn.

4.   Identify the last time a formal pricing training was conducted somewhere in your organization and access the content.

5.   Visit your training or HR professionals and investigate what it would take to design and launch basic pricing training programs over time to generate interest and visibility for pricing (in person or via webinar). You have to start somewhere!

6.   Volunteer to conduct "lunch and learn" events to give free training in pricing to a targeted group of professionals: marketing, sales, IT, and so on.

6 Change Capacity
A Progressive Internalization

The secret of change is to focus all your energy, not on fighting the old, but on building the new.

Dan Millman, *Way of the Peaceful Warrior*

In business, as in nature, nothing matters more than the ability to adapt. The individuals, departments, enterprises, industries, and even countries that manage change best tend to overtake entities that fail to adjust to new conditions. Pricing is no exception. Organizational change is at the heart of every pricing transformation. Without integrating the best change-management science in the pricing road map, your transformation program will have next to no chance of success.

This is old news to most pricing professionals, most of whom already know something about change. They often talk about change: every study, every panel discussion, and every talk touches on the importance of change. Nearly two thirds, 65 percent, have even taken a formal course in change management, according to a survey I conducted several years ago. However, they tend to focus mostly on the technical challenge and completely ignore the "soft" part of change management—getting people on board in a way that makes the change irreversible.

Unfortunately, few pricing experts realize that although installing the technology is important, a successful pricing transformation also demands modifying the organization's behavior, attitudes, and processes. Faced with uncertainty and complexity, managers tend to ignore the change-management challenge inherent in making a permanent change in a firm's pricing DNA (Forbis and Mehta 1981) and pricing orientation (Liozu et al. 2011). As pricing is considered a complex and sometimes political function (Lancioni,

Schau, and Smith 2005), firms are often reluctant to undertake the effort, and managers "throw in the towel" fairly early (Dolan and Simon 1996).

Nor have scholars encouraged companies to focus on the importance of organizational change management in pricing transformations. Academic pricing literature is silent about the critical role that change plays in the transformation of pricing orientation and how the organization's capacity for change may affect the path a firm takes on its journey toward pricing excellence (Liozu et al. 2011).

One reason for the collective silence may be that there is no easy formula. A "big bang" approach to pricing transformation almost never works. A company in a difficult competitive situation may have no choice but a crash pricing program. However, unlike the movies, where someone's "crazy plan that just might work" actually does work by the time the credits roll, crash pricing programs generally crash. All the anecdotes and case studies of the Professional Pricing Society about pricing transformations suggest the same thing: survivors of a disruptive transformation say the project had too many moving parts, moving in too many directions to accomplish anything but destroy morale.

The truth is that a pricing transformation requires the most difficult kind of change (as shown in Figure 6.1)—an evolution that is ongoing, incremental, and enterprise-wide. This is why the transformational model presented in Chapter 2 is also an incremental change model that is full of experimentation and iteration that allows firms to change slowly over time. This takes a lot more than a new price sheet and a pep talk. It's a multiyear, multistep, multiprocess, multidimensional journey. You make a change and then stop, make sure that the new process and new level of understanding is absorbed and adopted, and then move on to the next step. Like the old joke

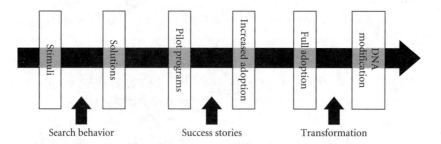

Figure 6.1 Incremental approach to change

About the Research

To test our hypotheses, I designed a cross-sectional self-administered survey to measure the latent variables associated with our conceptual model. The Professional Pricing Society (PPS) supported the survey by (1) providing access to their database of active members, (2) distributing the survey electronically, and (3) conducting follow-ups to nonrespondents. Characteristics of the respondents are provided in Table 6.1.

The society's marketing team sent an email to the members, followed by two reminder emails to encourage participation. Over 1,500 members responded. After removing all partial and incomplete responses, we deemed 939 survey responses acceptable for statistical analysis. The survey measured organizational change capacity using a 32-item scale developed by Judge and Douglas (2009). This measurement scale consisted of eight critical dimensions of change, each having four specific items to be rated. Respondents answered every question on a seven-point Likert scale anchored at the extremes by "strongly agree" and "strongly disagree."

Table 6.1 Sample characteristics

Nature	Count	Percentage	Function	Count	Percentage
B2B	761	81	General management	100	11
B2C	143	15	Marketing and sales	148	16
Not sure	35	4	Pricing and revenue management	631	67
Firm size	*Count*	*Percentage*	Others	60	6
Less than 1,000	215	23			
1,001 to 10,000	294	31	*Corporate pricing team*	*Count*	*Percentage*
Over 10,000	425	45	Yes	677	72
Not sure	5	1	No	243	26
			Not sure	19	2

NOTE: Firm size refers to the number of employees.

about how to get to Carnegie Hall ("Practice, practice, practice!"), there are no shortcuts to acquiring advanced pricing capabilities.

But there is change and there is change. All change is hard, but as I explain in the next section, academics say some kinds of change are harder to achieve than others.

What the Literature Is Telling Us

Change is hard. Studies show that approximately 70 percent of planned organizational change initiatives fail (Judge and Douglas 2009). Changes seldom succeed unless the organization is receptive (Butler 2003) and ready for the change (Holt et al. 2007), but building that consensus isn't easy. Most organizations tend to resist change—and the more successful the organization has been in the past, the harder it will resist. The work is so difficult that even management scholars have tended to shy away from the subject and focus instead on how to change the mind of an individual. Out of the hundreds of academic studies that address change management, few deal specifically with change where it matters most: at the organizational level.

Those few published studies that do concern organizational change focus mostly on how to cope with a particular event, which is not really the core pricing challenge. Although a pricing transformation includes events, it's really about driving a bigger, more comprehensive change in the entire operating environment. What matters more is to develop the capacity for ongoing, continuous evolution. Sufficiently developed, such a capacity for coping with change can become a strategic weapon that allows the firm to learn from changes in the environment and to exploit these changes by adjusting its own processes (Judge and Blocker 2008).

How successfully organizations handle change depends on a number of factors that Moilanen (2005:71) described as *organizational change capacity (OCC)*. Moilanen defined OCC as "a consciously managed organization with 'learning' as a vital component in its values, visions and goals, as well as its everyday operations and assessment." Extending this idea, Judge and Douglas (2009:635) proposed a combination of organizational and managerial capabilities that allows "an enterprise to adapt more quickly and effectively than its competition to changing situations." They divided organizational change capacity into five basic elements (Figure 6.2).

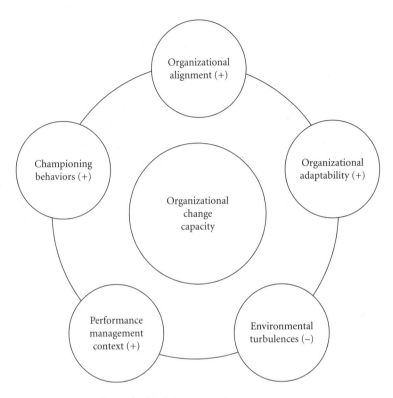

Figure 6.2 Antecedents of organizational change capacity

Organizational Ambidexterity (Alignment + Adaptability)

Organizations need to be able to find the right balance between adapting to environmental turbulences by embracing change and managing day-to-day and short-term operations (Birkinshaw and Gibson 2004). This balance between change and stability becomes even more important when firms embark on a process of deep and sustained change (Meyer and Stensaker 2006). Meyer and Stensaker (2006:228) propose that to build the capacity to change, "organizations need to balance between the need to implement changes, the need to maintain daily operations, and the need to implement changes in the future"—a combination of skills sometimes referred as ambidexterity.

Ambidexterity is difficult to achieve. Management systems often cause the firm to waste resources on unproductive activities. Nearly as negative is the fact that management systems tend to lead teams within the organization to work at cross-purposes by giving them conflicting objectives or by making it difficult to integrate systems in a way that encourages the teams to pull in the same direction.

Championing Behaviors

Top management plays a key role in defining and promoting corporate-wide priorities and new strategic programs and in identifying, allocating, and deploying strategic resources to support these programs (Chandler 1973:4). Most of the time, however, executives stand aside and simply monitor the process. Too many abdicate their responsibility and try to delegate it to someone else (Nadler 1997). These leaders expect that a "silver bullet will unlock the mysteries of organizational change" (Nadler 1997:10) but fail to recognize that they generally have to drive the change themselves by encouraging the entire organization (Kanter 1984).

Context

Champions play a pivotal role in establishing a proper performance management context, supporting the broader change mandate. A high-performance management context shapes the individual and collective behaviors that, over time, enable adaptability and alignment (Birkinshaw and Gibson 2004).

Respondents to my survey rated the ability of managers to use enterprise-wide goals to focus the objectives of their own unit, and to set their own challenging and aggressive goals as the most crucial behaviors. Stretch goals for change performance also seem to be important. However, my analysis suggests that the degree to which the company champions pricing correlates most closely to its pricing power, followed by its ability to encourage innovation and change and its capacity to support experimentation. Somewhat less important but still crucial is an ability to consistently articulate an inspiring view of the future and an ability to protect the company's core value while still encouraging change.

But they can't just be good at change. Organizations with a good capacity for change must demonstrate the ability to run daily operations and change initiatives at the same time. The business must continue whether change happens or not. Both sets of activities must be closely aligned with a proper pricing vision, aligned goals, and performance outcomes. Change champions need good interpersonal skills and show strong conviction, courage, and confidence about the changes they need to make.

Environmental Turbulences

Competitive intensity, market disruptions, and environmental turbulences can all slow the pace of change. The adoption of value-based pricing methods, for example, is an ongoing and dynamic process. As the customer-value assessment process requires the identification and evaluation of factors that differentiate a firm's products from those of the competition (Hinterhuber 2004; Nagle and Holden 2002), any changes in the competitors' product value proposition may affect the firm's customer value (Smith and Nagle 2005) or value equivalence (Leszinski and Marn 1997). In addition, changes in external dynamics may result in a general inability of the sector to understand the new situation. Managers can become overwhelmed by the amount of competitive information they need to digest and the number of pricing decisions they must make (Dutta, Zbaracki, and Bergen 2003). Competitive intensity can generate more stress, uncertainty, and "unanalyzability" of market information (Daft and Weick 1984), lead to a reduction in the ability to buffer against uncertainties (Lynn 2005), and potentially reduce the capacity for change (Judge and Douglas 2009). The levels of risk, turbulence, and rapid rate of obsolescence now common in many industries demand reaction times and a strong capability to respond adequately and in a timely manner.

But to do it, you first need to understand something about organizational change capacity.

Dimensions of Organizational Change Capacity

Clearly, culture, leadership style, leadership traits, and communication systems all affect change capacity. But which factors matter most? To find out, we borrowed the measurement scale of Judge and Douglas (2009), which defines organizational change capacity as 32 items organized in the following eight dimensions:

> *Trustworthy leaders.* Senior executives whom the rest of the organization trusts to show stakeholders how to meet their shared goals

Trusting followers. Nonexecutive employees who feel free to discuss and disagree with a new path advocated by a senior executive—and also, to ultimately adopt and follow the executive's plan

Capable champions. Empowered change leaders

Involved midmanagement. Middle managers who can effectively align the rest of the organization with senior leadership

Innovative culture. The ability of the organization to establish norms of innovation and encourage innovative activity

Accountable culture. The ability of the organization to carefully steward resources and meet deadlines

Effective communication. The ability of the organization to communicate vertically, horizontally, and with customers

Systems thinking. The ability of the organization to focus on root causes and recognize the interdependencies within and outside its boundaries

All eight dimensions are important, but in my survey of 939 pricing professionals conducted in 2012, I found that my colleagues considered some qualities much more important than others (Table 6.2). When I asked pricing professionals what factors mattered most in a pricing transformation (on a scale of 1 to 7 with 7 being "strongly agree" and 1 "strongly disagree"), most agreed that capable champions, solid systems thinking, and a culture of accountability are the three most important factors—in that order.

All of these results correspond with what I have seen in the field. First, having a champion for the transformation is crucial. To succeed with a pricing transformation, not only must the organization have an enthusiastic senior executive committed to leading the charge, but this leader must understand the dynamics of change management and recognize the special role a leader plays in any successful transformation. Their instinct about the second-most significant factor seems correct to me as well: the ability to see the interrelationships between all the parts of the system. Successful transformational leaders have a deep understanding of all the moving parts that will be changed by the organization and their underlying interrelationships. Finally, accountability is crucial: individuals must be held accountable for their role in the change. Debate leading up to the transformation

Table 6.2 Dimensions of organizational change capacity

Dimensions of change capacity	Average score
Capable champions	**4.99**
Systems thinking	**4.89**
Accountable culture	**4.87**
Trustworthy leaders	4.78
Involved midmanagement	4.78
Trusting followers	4.64
Innovative culture	4.57
Effective communication	4.33
In this organization, change champion(s) . . . (dimension: capable champions)	Average
Possess good interpersonal skills	5.11
Have the will and creativity to bring about change	5.04
Are willing and able to challenge the status quo	4.99
Command the respect of the rest of the organization	4.79
Dimension average	*4.98*
In this organization, change champions recognize . . . (dimension: systems thinking)	Average
The importance of institutionalizing change	5.09
The value of addressing causes rather than symptoms	4.92
The systems implications of change	4.81
The need to realign incentives with desired changes	4.73
Dimension average	*4.89*
In this organization, employees . . . (dimension: accountable culture)	Average
Accept responsibility for getting work done	5.24
Meet deadlines and honor resource commitments	5.00
Have clear roles for who has to do what	4.62
Experience consequences for outcomes of their actions	4.61
Dimension average	*4.87*

is healthy, but once the work begins, resistance must stop. A handful of unhappy employees can obstruct the work of the entire team. Sooner or later, everyone in the organization must be converted to the cause—or removed.

The strength of the innovation culture ranked seventh, a fact many executives should find encouraging, as it suggests that even a subgenius company can succeed in pricing. Nor did systems communication matter much—although this factor, ironically, is the change skill that pricing consultants tend to focus on most.

Once the change is made, the next question is, how do you make it stick? Most transformations offer plenty of opportunities to go back to the old ways and to stop progressing. When do you know that change is here to stay? How do you maintain new behaviors over time?

Transformational and Irreversible Change

The implementation and internalization of pricing knowledge requires deep organizational changes that will transform the fabric of a firm's life and identity as well as the identity of its members. This transformation is not just a matter of adding a new module to the enterprise resource planning system or a new pricing schedule to the reps' sales kits. Instead, pricing adoption requires a slow "mutation" of what participants in my research studies called their "firm DNA." Although this shift away from a focus on prices based on cost or competition to prices based on customer value must eventually include the cooperation of the entire organization, it generally begins with the pricing team and then moves on to sales.

Sales cooperation is vital. Most firms underestimate the sales team's tendency to resist pricing structure changes and their power to block or derail pricing initiatives. In my experience, the only way to overcome their resistance is to do the following:

- *Get sales involved from day one.* Your reps should be included in the road map design, strategy discussions, brainstorming sessions, blueprinting, meetings with pricing vendors, customer interviews, and more.

- *Avoid surprises.* By getting sales leaders actively involved in the various programs of the transformation early on and keeping them involved, the sales team will be much more likely to go along with whatever happens next.

- *Communicate a vision and a road map.* To be a good accountant or logistics person for your company, you don't necessarily need to believe in your company's offering. But to be a good sales rep, you must be able to convince people outside the organization that your offering is best—and that means you must be either a great actor or a true believer—and preferably the latter. A lack of alignment about the pricing strategy can deeply undermine this kind of faith. Sales teams hate having to deal with too many uncertainties and a lack of strategic direction. Explaining why, when, and how things are going to happen may not win them over, but it will help keep your debate focused on real issues rather than rumors and conjectures.

- *Focus on* "What is in it for me?" To the individual, the organization's priorities are always secondary. Buy-in for any new program or process is always easier when the individual understands how it will help him.
- *Conduct brainstorming sessions with the sales force.* Asking a series of questions, such as (1) "How truly differentiated are we?," (2) "What's preventing you from being successful today in value selling?," or (3) "What did you learn today and what did it mean to you?," can all help reduce griping and anxiety. Brainstorm sessions in which the pricing team are the only outsiders can also be a great opportunity to let reps ventilate and speak frankly about the challenges they face internally and externally.

However, you need more than the sales team on your side if you want to change the entire culture. You must get everybody on board, including finance, marketing, innovation, customer service, and the supply chain. Your entire company must be fully aligned with the pricing program.

Such a change requires intense and sustained organizational mobilization to transform the previously established structure, culture, processes, and systems. Marketers, sellers, and developers have to change their business mentality and their frames of reference and embrace new value-related concepts as a new "way of life" (Forbis and Mehta 1981). They must also learn a new language that enables them to carry the value message internally and externally. In a company committed to a value-based pricing future, people must become "organizational pricing heroes" or leave the organization before they hold back the rest of the team.

One key characteristic of organizations that know how to manage change well is their ability to learn (Weick and Sutcliffe 2007) from their successes and their failures.

As I mentioned in Chapter 3, two kinds of learning must be mastered by any organization that hopes to transform its pricing practices, the same ones we use to learn anything: experiential learning and transformative learning. Each has pluses and minuses.

Learning through experience relies on case studies, experiments, and pilot studies (Kolb 1984; Kolb, Boyatzis, and Mainemelis 2001; Pfeffer and Sutton 2006). The innovative, subjective, and sometimes contentious nature of pricing changes usually leads people all over the company to modify their frames of reference, learning patterns, and vocabulary to accommodate the integration of new and progressive pricing knowledge. It's all about trial and error, the development and delivery of success stories, the celebration of wins and recognition, and the analysis of failures. The advantage of experiential learning is that what employees learn in this way can't really be questioned, a fact that tends to speed adoption. When you say, "We rolled out this pilot and at the end of the pilot, our profits grew 15 percent," executives are much more likely to be convinced about the value of a larger rollout than anything you can point to in a theoretical paper. The disadvantage is that these kinds of demonstrations can take a long time and force you to reinvent the wheel over and over.

Transformational learning is more of a conversion process. Rather than learn only from your own experiments, you learn to copy others' successes and avoid their mistakes. This demands changing a mind-set and frames of reference, role-playing with peers, coaching, learning the language of value, and reinforcing behavioral changes—a process that tends to be more on the order of working with a mentor than experiential learning. Whereas experiential learning changes minds, transformational learning changes hearts (Figure 6.3).

Both forms of learning play an important role in any transformation. Experiential learning will be most convincing to leaders, but its significance may be less persuasive to ordinary employees. Transformational learning, on the other hand, with its focus on relationships and emotion, can be more convincing to the rank and file. Obviously, each form can reinforce the other.

The best thing is to teach both ways and ensure that all pricing users and setters receive a similar education in pricing. As pricing users and setters experiment, role-play, learn by doing, and interact in groups, they absorb new concepts, techniques, methods, and roles. Behaviors change as they do things over and over in training workshops and then in real life. Behavior modification over time makes those changes irreversible. But old habits die hard. Some of these changes can take as long as 18 to 24 months. Both experiential and transformative training programs should start at the beginning of the transformation and keep going. And no matter how good the

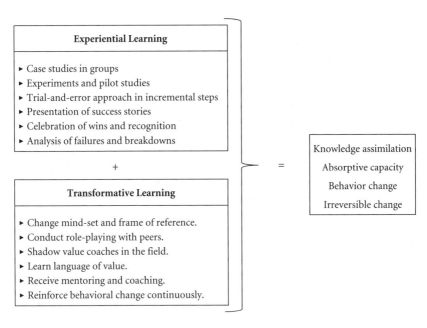

Figure 6.3 Learning to change

organization gets, everyone must keep learning. Even championship teams have coaches.

Most change-management methodologies (Prosci, Kotter, and LaMarsh Global, for example) emphasize the importance of reinforcing change after installing pricing assets and after executing pricing activities (Liozu 2014). We consider the most important reinforcement methods next.

Dimensions of Transformational Change in Pricing

Recognizing the critical role of change in my 5C model of transformation, I wanted to learn whether established change-management methodologies could be applied to pricing transformations. To find out, I first became certified in the Prosci ADKAR change methodology and studied five other change methodologies in depth: the Kotter Change Model, the LaMarsh Managed Change method, the McKinsey 7S change framework, Boyatzis's Intentional Change Theory, and Bohn's Organization Change Process. Combining the insights of these change-management methodologies with

- Strategic organizational alignment
- CEO championing behaviors
- Executive sponsorship
- Communicated pricing vision
- Simple pricing transformational road map
- Holistic "what is in it for me" analysis
- Thorough stakeholder analysis
- Change- and project-management collaboration
- Dedicated program to build organizational confidence
- Visualizing pricing success: before, during, and after

Transformational intelligence

Figure 6.4 Critical dimensions of transformational change

my academic research and experience, I found ten dimensions of transformational change that matter in pricing, as shown in Figure 6.4.

These ten dimensions are a toolbox of methods, approaches, and specific exercises that can significantly boost an organization's transformational intelligence when it embarks on a pricing transformation. Some are fairly intuitive, such as vision and communication. Others are essential to build organizational buy-in for the project, such as analyses for the individual ("*What is in it for me?*") and the stakeholder ("*What's in it for them?*").

Strategic organizational alignment. We have mentioned before the importance of aligning different business units across the enterprise for generating organizational buy-in, but alignment matters for other reasons as well. How many firms have value-oriented strategies but volume-oriented incentives systems? How many times have you heard conflicting instructions between top and middle management? The front lines are quick to spot goals that are aimed at cross-purposes—and quick to take advantage of the confusion. If directions, guidelines, and instructions are confusing and contradictory, they can easily derail the execution of the pricing programs and pricing tactics. Alignment is needed to demonstrate the role of pricing in the larger business strategy and to explain the overall pricing philosophy to the whole hierarchy of the business.

CEO championing of pricing. This book includes a chapter on the role of the CEO as a champion of the pricing transformation. In this case, championing does not necessarily mean acting as the executive sponsor of the overall transformation but rather acting as its "chief energizing officer." My research shows a positive and significant relationship between the CEO's championing of pricing and firm performance.

Executive sponsoring. Cynics say success has many fathers, but in pricing, this remark is actually true. A fundamental component of change-management success seems to be the support of several executive sponsors. These sponsors must be high enough in the hierarchy to have clout, decision-making authority, or at least access to the top decision maker. Such heavyweights ensure that all project and change components stay on track, on budget, and on target. At the same time, they need to be somewhat above the fray; they should not be involved in the day-to-day tactics of the change process, but they need to be in a position to nudge middle managers along. They act as the relay between the top layers of the organization and the people doing the work. They should be able to provide guidance, leadership, and coaching to the project directors as well as to the change managers. The combination of a CEO championing the pricing transformation and strong operational executive sponsors can work wonders in driving a pricing transformation forward.

Communicated pricing vision. Executing a pricing transformation without a clear and crisp pricing vision in place would be difficult, if not impossible. You will remember that 66 percent of the CEOs I surveyed in 2011 admitted they lacked a clearly defined corporate pricing vision. This is a stunning admission, given that without that vision, advanced pricing is almost impossible to adopt. In an advanced company, the vision will include a statement of the primary orientation that the organization needs to follow not only when it sets prices but also to provide direction for how the organization should execute its pricing program—a mantra that should be included on the second page of every PowerPoint presentation relating to the pricing transformation, set in large type and Technicolor. People need to know that their leaders care about the project. One of the things I always recommend to my clients is to brand the pricing transformational project with a logo, a tagline, and a road map outlining the stages of the transformation, as a way to help create an image of the project and to develop awareness, and use the branding in the overall communication plan.

A simple road map. Stakeholders participating in the project need to see a simple road map that shows how the organization will get there. I am a true believer in simple but powerful visuals to generate interest and buy-in from employees, especially people unused to corporate programs or intimidated by them. This visual should be posted in all project presentations to constantly remind the team of where they are and where they are going. The operative word is *simple.* Too many times, corporate experts make things too complicated for people to grasp—and obviously, when someone doesn't understand a program, chances are good he won't be able to follow its guidelines. The road map should be easily understood and not use any technical jargon that may intimidate stakeholders. You may be able to break down the pricing road map into distinct horizons to avoid this common pitfall: people are scared of too much change at once. Showing them a five- to seven-year road map can soothe their concerns.

Thorough stakeholder analysis. The pricing road map should include all relevant stakeholders who may participate in or be affected by the pricing transformation. All change-management consultants say mapping the stakeholders is a crucial first step in change management, and I believe this is also true for a pricing transformation. This analysis should include every function that touches, creates, sets, modifies, teaches, or communicates pricing. Usually, pricing leaders remember to include pricing, marketing, sales, and finance, but frequently overlook technical support, customer service, innovation, operations, and training. However, my experience in pricing transformation shows that the more functions that pricing leaders involve in the stakeholder analysis, the better their odds of success. Some functions may have limited involvement in the overall project. Others will be central to it. But whatever the nature and degree of the impact, all functions should be brought formally into the project, trained in pricing, and assigned a clear role. This helps create organizational buy-in and a strong sense of alignment.

Holistic "What is in it for me?" analysis. This is probably the most important piece of the pricing transformation puzzle and of the change-management tool kit. Every stakeholder needs to understand not only what parts of their work will change but why they should embrace it. Take the time to explain to them why they should support the project and how they will benefit. This creates a positive vision for them and for their future. Adding one or two slides to the overall training programs and repeating targeted messages about the value of the transformation to particular individuals can go a long way toward building enthusiasm. The role of the CEO and the executive sponsor can make a big difference here, especially in reassuring the sales force. I recently conducted such a training program with 50 sales representatives of a privately owned firm in which I included the *"What is in it for me?"* analysis at the front end of my presentation. I showed them how their role would evolve over the next two years, emphasizing the overall advantages that better pricing would bring them and the firm. The result: hope and a positive attitude toward change. They also accepted that the need for change was real and that their role would be critical. I came away feeling more certain than ever that when you embark on a pricing transformation, you should do a *"What is in it for me?"* analysis as soon as possible. You will learn things along the way and will undoubtedly need to modify those initial statements to reflect what you've learned, but it's important to start with that optimistic image. All along the journey, keep reminding them of why you are making the changes. People tend to forget.

Change- and project-management collaboration. Some firms have dedicated project-management and change-management teams. Overlapping areas of responsibility should be kept to a minimum. Communication between the teams should be constant, in order to make sure that the plans reinforce each other and don't work at cross-purposes. Top executives also need to understand each team's role in the transformation. Such parameters can be well defined from the beginning; generally speaking, project managers take charge of the various pricing project implementations, and change mangers make sure the firm does not neglect the psychological and behavioral dimensions of the project.

In small and medium firms, pricing professionals may wear both change and project manager hats. Although more challenging, that challenge is not insurmountable. I strongly believe that you do not need an army of change managers to conduct a pricing transformation. If pricing professionals receive proper foundational training in change-management methodologies and include some of the critical elements presented in this chapter in their transformational plan, the company doesn't necessarily need a separate change manager.

Dedicated program to build organization confidence. Most pricing projects include basic training programs on common pricing issues, such as value, pricing, and negotiation. But it's not enough. Many companies ignore this critical dimension of the transformation, but boosting the perceived collective power of teams can create a sense of "can-do" and collective resilience. This cannot be underestimated as an important element of transformation change. In Chapter 7, I propose a toolbox with 24 programs that can be selected and used to boost the level of organizational confidence.

Visualizing pricing success. Finally, teams should be presented with visual statements of the pricing system before, during, and after the transformation. Early on in the book, I indicated that firms usually conduct transformations in order to solve a serious business problem related to pricing. But the organization won't be able to do that if employees don't recognize what the problem or problems are and understand in concrete terms what will happen during the transformation. One way to do this is to create another visual showing a before, a during, and an after situation. The organization needs to be given a vision of future success that will generate a hopeful, optimistic attitude. Hope relates closely to the "*What is in it for me?*" analysis. Generally speaking, hope creates an emotional connection with the transformational project, and an emotional connection helps drive buy-in. Without an emotional connection, there can be no transformation (Fredrickson 2009; Boyatzis and McKee 2005). One last element that makes a tremendous difference in the change process is to measure how the organization is doing against the desired states. Pricing leaders need to define the relevant measures of change success and to communicate progress regularly. That includes rate of adoption, proficiency levels on new software or tools, levers of price performance, and more. Having a cockpit widely available that people can use to see the progress as it is made can be a powerful tool for reinforcing optimism about the transformation.

What's in a Name?

To be successful in the early stages of a change initiative, think hard about the name of the project you are about to manage and the nature of the overall transformation. For instance, you may not even want to include pricing in your project name. The P-word comes with some negative baggage. I have seen talk of pricing derail initiatives time and time again. First, the pricing leader starts talking about the new *pricing* initiative, and then everyone in the room begins to squirm and find reasons not to do it. I suspect people often associate a pricing project with quantitative work and analytics—not a favorite activity for most. My first recommendation when I meet with project teams is to immediately change the name of the project to something no one can have an objection to, such as *customer value* or *marketing excellence*. This may sound like a trivial point in the overall discussion, but when you are dealing with emotional and sometimes irrational individuals, the last thing you want to do is use an upsetting word over and over. Calling a transformational project a *value excellence* or *marketing excellence* project not only tends to be better received, but it's more accurate in that it represents the larger impact of a successful pricing transformation project.

I've seen this phenomenon firsthand. I advised the leaders of a pricing transformation project for a company in Atlanta that lasted 24 months. Although originally sold as a pricing project, this pricing transformation ended up encompassing business model innovation, value discovery processes, strategic renewal, and strategic alignment and compensation systems. During this project, I had to repeat consistently and constantly, even to top executives, why we were doing work that at first glance looked far removed from pricing. "What has this to do with pricing?" and "How do we apply this to pricing?" were questions that kept coming back from the CEO and other executives. I had to explain that the nature of the pricing problems and their root causes required us to go deeper in some unexpected dimensions, including business model and corporate strategy. After that, we quickly renamed the initiative a *customer value* project to make sure that the scope reflected the type of work we were conducting. This is typical. Most of the time, the transformation will not just be a simple pricing project. It will require other changes as well. Avoid the "P-word" and you'll have an easier time bringing people on board.

The Language of Value and Change

Another change that can help improve the odds of success is to use a positive vocabulary that ignites people's spirit and motivation. Here is a real example from a recent conversation with a pricing leader rewritten in transformational terms:

From: "We do not pay attention to profit leaks and do not control the erratic discounting behavior of sales force. We do not price on value and we use cost-based pricing too much, and as a result we leave money on the table."

To: "Our intention is to improve the importance of customer value in how we price our product and service so that we can capture more value in the market and identify areas of profit opportunities and reduced leakage. The sales force plays a significant role in the success of our pricing programs, and it is our responsibility to bring them on board."

Let us do a quick analysis of words in the first sentence:

- Words with negative connotations: *not* (3), *leaks, control, erratic, discounting, cost, too much, leave* = 10 words.
- Words with positive connotations: *profit, value* = 2 words.

Let us do the same exercise for the words in the second sentence:

- Words with negative connotations: *reduced, leakage* = 2 words.
- Words with positive connotations: *improve, value* (2), *capture, more, profit, opportunities, significant, success, on board* = 10 words.

Positive words create energy, hope, and confidence, while negative words tend to reinforce negative patterns and resistance to change (Fredrickson 2009). Over time, the ratio of positive to negative words can make a significant difference to the company's DNA. I am not the only one to say this. One study that counted word frequencies in the speeches of the most charismatic change leaders in the history of humankind (Mahatma Gandhi, Martin Luther King, Nelson Mandela, Bill Clinton, Charles de Gaulle, Mother Teresa, etc.) found that those leaders' positive words far outweighed the negative. Some of the best behavioral scientists in the world, including Coleman, Boyatzis, and Fredrickson, recommend a ratio of five positive words to every one negative word (Boyatzis and McKee 2005).

So what does that mean for pricing and marketing practitioners? It means that you have to be aware and mindful of the words you use, particularly the ratio of positive to negative words, when you are trying to change behaviors in teams. I am not saying you can no longer use some of the words listed in Table 6.3. The main point is to have a balance in the words you use and how you use them. Recently, one pricing leader from Hewlett-Packard made this comment while presenting his pricing journey: "They were scared of losing their job to machines. Because of this we had to energize them and be super-enthusiastic."

When crafting communication strategies to support pricing projects and change programs, practitioners should make the effort to use a greater number of positive words regarding value and change. Value stories and critical value messages also have to be positive and hopeful. They have to use the customer language and carry a vision of success, pride, and accomplishment. The easy way to ensure this is to analyze your messages and presentations as we did earlier in this chapter. Your marketing communications experts can help you with the process, especially when you build value stories and communication material for change.

Table 6.3 The power of words

Positive words	Negative words
Customer	Cost
Benefits	Control
Value	Discount
Success	Decrease
Improvement	Cutting
Increase	Problem
Boost	Erosion

Conclusion: Pricing Practitioners Need to Be Change Agents

Perhaps the most difficult part of managing the change is to get the organization to accept that the transformation will never be over and pricing will never go back to "normal." Once value-based pricing is adopted, the days of nearly unconscious, automatic price setting never return. Plus, value-based pricing changes the customer relationship, the company's value proposition, and the identity of the company. The pricing executive's role now becomes strategic and perhaps even visionary.

Nor does it end there. As pricing executives will show their colleagues, pricing means a more conscious life not just for the pricing function, but for marketing, finance, and the organization as a whole. It's not easy. The bigger the change, the greater the complexity of meeting that challenge. As one executive told me, "I don't think it happens overnight. It's a journey. It's a journey with multiple, multiple small steps, and [we have] been on this journey for a while. A lot of progress was made, but the journey is not complete. We've got a ways to go, but there's a lot of energy behind it" (Liozu et al. 2011).

Change Capacity: Some Tips to Get Started

1. The pricing leader should train herself in change management and/or obtain some certification in change management. This will increase her internal credibility as a change agent.

2. Change managers should do two critical things right away: the "*What is in it for me?*" analysis and stakeholder analysis.

3. Do not call your pricing transformational project a pricing project. Call it a marketing or customer excellence project. Focus on branding and messaging of the project.

4. Identify important allies in the organization who could help and support the initiative. Make sure these people eventually become executive sponsors.

5. Conduct an organizational change capacity survey to assess your organization's capacity to take on a pricing journey. Use the first assessment as a benchmark and then repeat the survey process every 12 to 15 months to gauge progress.

7 Confidence
The Fuel of the Organizational Transformation

Selling is essentially a transference of feeling.

Zig Ziglar, *Secrets of Closing the Sale*

Henry Ford once said, "Whether you think you can or you think you can't—you're right." This is definitely true for pricing. In my experience— and I have confirmed this through research—one of the biggest predictors of success in a pricing transformation is the level of confidence the members of the organization have that they can complete difficult large-scale projects. And it is why I present this *C* in last position. Confidence is the gel that brings all the rest of the *C*s together—it's the fuel of organizational transformation.

Organizational confidence relates to a sense of "can-do" (Hinterhuber and Liozu 2012) and group self-esteem (Bohn 2001). Imagine two kickoff meetings for a hard project that the organization is about to take on. People in one room are asking themselves: Can we do it? As a team, can we pull this off? The other group, meanwhile, feels that they face a challenge but not an impossible one. In my experience, this latter group tends to be the one that succeeds. It's as if by imagining a light at the end of the tunnel, they create an end to the tunnel.

This is particularly true for pricing. When an organization is about to take a difficult step in the pricing transformation, it must have a strong be- lief not only in the value of the project but in the company's business model and long-term strategy. The pricing project must fit an overall vision that makes sense to everyone. Business leaders should pay particular attention to encouraging the team's beliefs in the company business model and the quality of the offering. It takes more than guts to resist a customer's request for a deal, or to trust that your story is strong enough that you don't have to meet a competitor's price cut. It takes conviction. A sales team won't be able to resist the pressure if they don't believe their price is deserved; an individual might bluff, but confidence in an organization depends on a fundamental level of self-assurance. As one executive at a company that successfully implemented value-based pricing told me, "You have to have a culture [where] the people inside believe that what you're doing is better than the next guy, that you're using better ingredients, that you have better technology behind the product formulation."

But what is confidence, really? We know it when we see it and when we feel it, but to understand what confidence is, let's take a bit of a dive in the literature.

What the Literature Is Telling Us

Management thinkers are still trying to figure out what factors make an organization confident, but some now suggest that it can be understood best by looking at social cognitive theory and the concept of self-efficacy.

Social cognitive theory (Bandura 1997) suggests that people participate in organizations either because they believe in themselves or because they believe in the organization, in the "individual's perception of his or her ability to perform generic teamwork behavior (self-efficacy) and perceptions regarding the team's ability to complete the task (collective efficacy)" (Tasa, Taggar, and Seijts 2007). A meta-analysis conducted by Gully et al. (2002) showed that the relationship between collective confidence and team performance was positive and significant, supporting social cognitive theory's holding that efficacy is "a primary determinant to the extent to which individuals or teams are likely to put the efforts required to perform successfully" (Bandura 1986:392).[1] In other words, when we don't believe, we may keep punching the clock, but we have already gone home. We're in the world of Dilbert and The Office—a place where zombie workers go through the motions, feel that making a genuine commitment to their work is a sucker's game, and ultimately make their nightmare come true.

Notice that I have not mentioned anything about market share or pricing power. The crucial issue is to make sure that employees believe in their individual capacities and in their organization's competence and understand that their own interests align with their company's interest. Fortunately, pricing leaders can do something about each of those factors.

Dimensions of Collective Confidence in Pricing

How do you build collective confidence? You might imagine it would be primarily a function of market power—or failing that, pure chutzpah. In fact, the answer does not have a lot to do with either the quality of the offering or the audacity of your sales reps. Confidence in pricing isn't something an organization inherits. It's an attitude that can be nurtured through behavior. In this chapter, we will review why I think that's the case and look at 24 tactics that some of the world's leading pricing experts use to boost their company's confidence levels. These programs are organized around the six dimensions of organizational confidence that emerged through my research (Figure 7.1): experimentation, recognition, communication, rationality, incentives, and people. Undertaking these relevant activities can positively boost the level of organizational confidence in pricing and value selling, and in turn influence firm performance. (For more details about the survey, see "About the Research.")

In a confident organization, these six dimensions act together as an engine that boosts the organization's belief systems. They work in concert to

Figure 7.1 Dimensions of organizational confidence in pricing

About the Research

Following our qualitative research process, Andreas Hinterhuber and I designed a cross-sectional self-administered survey. We surveyed commercial, sales, and account management professionals and leaders involved in conducting and managing pricing activities for their firms. The Strategic Account Management Association (SAMA), a professional organization dedicated to the education and networking of strategic account managers around the world, supported our research by providing access to their database of active members, distributing the survey electronically, and following up with nonrespondents. We emailed the survey to 7,200 SAMA members in June 2011. Responses were returned over a six-week period. A total of 723 surveys were returned partially or fully completed for a response rate of 10.3 percent. We determined that 507 surveys were usable for further analysis. Characteristics of the respondents are provided in Table 7.1.

To determine the level of organizational confidence in the respondents' organizations, we broke the survey into segments that assessed their sense of collective capability (4 items), sense of mission and future (4 items), and sense of resilience (4 items) using seven-point Likert scales anchored with "strongly agree" at the extreme positive end and "strongly disagree" at the opposite end of the scale. The

Table 7.1 Sample description

Main activity	Count	Percentage	Position of leadership (Y/N)	Count	Percentage
Manufacturing firm	306	60	Yes	346	68
Service organization	166	33	No	153	30
Distribution/retail company	30	6	Missing	8	2
Not sure	5	1	Respondent's location	Count	Percentage
Firm size	Count	Percentage	North America	314	62
Less than 250	77	15	Latin America	13	3
251 to 500	42	8	Europe	115	23
501 to 1,000	48	9	Asia Pacific	41	8
1,001 to 10,000	138	27	Middle East/Africa	16	3
More than 10,000	197	39	Not sure	8	2
Not sure	5	1	Total respondents	507	

NOTE: Firm size refers to the number of employees.

twelve-item scale was based on adapting existing measures from Bohn (2001). We asked,

To what extent do you agree or disagree with the following statements about your organization? (1 = strongly disagree to 7 = strongly agree)

1. We can take on any challenge.
2. Because our departments work together well, we can beat our competition.
3. We are more innovative than most organizations I have worked in.
4. Everyone works together effectively.
5. People here have a sense of purpose to accomplish something.
6. We have a strong vision of the future.
7. We are very certain about what we will accomplish together as a company.
8. We are confident about our future.
9. We believe in the value of our products/services.
10. We have the necessary courage to stand firm to customers' pricing objections.
11. We have the necessary courage to implement difficult price changes in the market.
12. We have a strong sense of resilience with pricing.

reach everyone in the organization who needs to be involved in a pricing transformation, from a truck driver delivering goods to customers to the vice president of technology who might be working at developing the next generation of exciting products. These dimensions also touch on some of the most sensitive aspects of human development: recognition, incentives, and communication. They may seem very commonsense to you, but I have seen the power of the 24 programs we are about to discuss. And they can make a huge difference in getting people on board and in succeeding in changing behaviors.

Confidence Is All About Collective Beliefs

Of course, success in pricing is a matter not only of a belief in pricing, but of belief in the organization itself (Figure 7.2). To succeed with any large project, employees need to feel they have the collective power and the

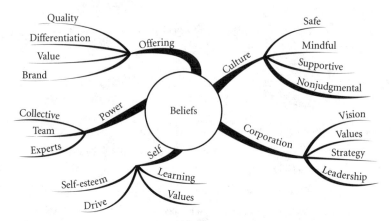

Figure 7.2 Organizational belief system

ability to meet their goals. To a great extent, a company's success often hinges on employees' ability to believe in the offering, their company, their company's culture, and finally, themselves.

This is particularly true for pricing. For a pricing transformation to succeed, employees must believe in the quality of their product—its differentiation, its value, and the integrity of their brand. Sales reps who aren't convinced that their offering is special will not be able to stick to a price and will be more inclined to "fold" under pressure from customers. They also need to feel that the offering is fair; it is important that employees feel that customers are being given a good value and that the company is working to make it even better. Pricing will not work in an atmosphere of cynicism. If the reps have the attitude that they are going "to put lipstick on the pig," any pricing improvements won't last long. As one executive told me, "You have to look [customers] in the eye and say, 'Ours costs more. This costs more, and it's worth it. You should pay more for that.' You have to be pretty confident to do that."

Employees need to believe in the company too, and have a sense that its values, vision, and strategy all make sense—and that its leaders have the capacity to inspire the company to fulfill that strategy. The culture needs to provide employees with positive support as well. They need to feel that they work in a safe, mindful, supportive, and nonjudgmental organization. At the same time, they need to sense some backbone in the hierarchy, and feel that the team, the experts, and the organization as a whole have the power to enforce their goals. Finally, at a personal level, they need to have the self-esteem, values, drive, and understanding to stick to the discipline that sophisticated pricing demands.

Whatever training and coaching it takes to achieve these positive attitudes is worth the investment. In my research, I have found a strong correlation between profit and confidence. Of course, correlation is not causation, but I don't think it's a coincidence that all the firms I interviewed that use value-based pricing have strong beliefs in their firm's products, technologies, and values. These beliefs help give sales staff and anyone who has interactions with customers the courage to stand firm to customers' pricing objections and to be, as one respondent stated, "Superman for one second" when facing customers' objections. CEOs and top executives in firms that embarked on a value transformation seemed to be most aware of the criticality of developing these internal beliefs (four out of four) and implemented specific programs and activities to boost organizational confidence. Three out of four firms using value-based pricing focused on specific people-development activities such as coaching sales staff and designing specific performance-management programs and talent-development plans around value orientation. We did not observe any cost-based pricing firms doing this, and only a minority of the firms that used cost-plus pricing did so.

The implementation and internalization of positive pricing attitudes is a long, tenuous, and sometimes painful journey of change for the entire organization. It requires an intense and sustained organizational mobilization to transform the established structure, culture, processes, and systems. Marketers, sellers, trainers, and anyone in contact with customers must change their business mentality and their frames of reference and embrace new value-related concepts that are expected to become a new "way of life" (Forbis and Mehta 1981). Everyone must learn a new language that enables them to carry the value message internally and externally. And I mean everyone: in a successful transformation, everyone must eventually change and become an "organizational hero" or leave the organization. As one vice president of global sales and marketing told us:

> We put people on performance reviews . . . the guy who was number one in targeted attainment three years ago was number three in sales target attainment last year . . . And he's on performance plan right now. The reason he's on a

performance plan is because he's at the bottom of the barrel on [value sell-ing]. . . . We said to him, "This isn't acceptable. I can get anyone to look after the [equipment] side. What I need someone is to change the market." . . . We've released a couple of people who haven't been able to make the transition, which has been difficult . . . That kind of performance management alignment is key.

Our research suggests that firms engaging in pricing transformations should intentionally design programs focused on building organizational confidence to accelerate members' buy-in and boost motivation levels to accept change. When confidence is high, people share beliefs in their "col-lective power" to produce desired outcomes and ends (Bohn 2001). Most studies have found a positive relationship between collective confidence and team performance (Gully et al. 2002).

But pricing confidence isn't a pill you swallow. Instead, it requires a fun-damental change in the organization's identity. As one executive told me, the journey to value-based pricing is a journey with "multiple small steps."

Value-Capture Confidence Revolution

To understand how pricing confidence can be cultivated, my colleague An-dreas Hinterhuber and I designed and executed a series of research projects over a four-year period that built on the existing body of work published in both academic and practitioner literature. One of these projects consisted of sixteen interviews with some of the best pricing leaders in the world. These leaders were all top pricing executives of organizations known for their progressive pricing programs. We wanted to find out what they had done to boost the organizational confidence of their teams, including their commercial teams. Based on the findings from these interviews, we were able to derive the six dimensions of organizational confidence and to ex-tract 24 specific initiatives, each of which can help boost at least one of those dimensions (Figure 7.3).

Twenty-four programs may seem like a lot, but more than half of these are already in place in most organizations. Most organizations already use some of them indirectly in their commercial excellence programs and/or their organizational development process. What is unique in this program is the idea of taking a holistic approach to boost collective confidence with

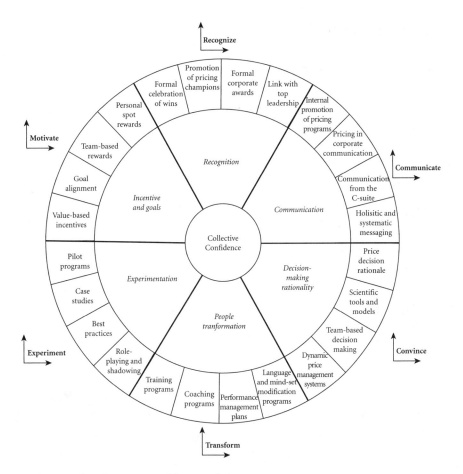

Figure 7.3 The value capture confidence revolution

respect to a particular project. Some of these initiatives require additional resources up front, while others will most likely just call for a slight modification of your company's existing processes and programs.

Often, it takes a while to persuade these leaders not to focus exclusively on the sales force. However, anyone in the organization who has customer contact should be included. From delivery drivers to the CEO, everyone needs to be touched by the change process. And this is where the confidence program starts to become powerful. I have used this confidence revolution methodology over the past 24 months to train business and sales leaders in several organizations on the concept of collective self-esteem and confidence in pricing and value management, and I have found that training everyone on critical dimensions of the value and pricing programs is a good idea. This democratic approach creates a sense of collective power that enables the entire organization to begin to convince itself that the new prices are justified. The approach resonates with the senior leaders I speak to as they eventually see how essential it is to transform the DNA of their entire organization.

1. Recognize

Recognition is a critical way to build the confidence of important players in a pricing transformation. This can be done at the individual level, at the team level, and at the department or enterprise level. Handled well, there is no limit to what recognition can achieve; to paraphrase Napoleon, it's difficult to hire a man to fight for you, but you can get him to risk his life for a bit of colored ribbon. There are any number of ways to give people the kind of recognition that will help turn a supporter into a champion (Table 7.2).

Table 7.2 Specific actions for the recognition dimension

Programs	Specific actions
Formal celebrations	Celebrate successes when projects go well or thresholds are reached.
	Promote and celebrate quick wins in pricing and value programs.
	Include wins and celebrations in the formal recognition and reward program.
	Hold one event per quarter to report wins related to the pricing transformation.
Promoting pricing champions	Identify pricing champions who are adopting pricing changes and are difference makers.
	Include a picture of pricing champions in corporate newsletters.
	Recognize pricing champions by inviting them to meet with executive sponsors.
Formal corporate awards	Create a Pricing Champion of the Year award.
	Hold a nomination and peer voting process for the award.
	Hold a formal award ceremony as part of corporate events.
Linking with top leadership	Elevate pricing champions and show their specific contribution to the C-suite.
	Organize personal lunch meetings between the CEO and pricing champions.
	Design a special award from the C-suite for outstanding pricing achievement.

Not only that, but pricing experts say it also instills a healthy level of competition as people vie to be the recipient next time.

2. Motivate

Don't expect people to just "do things." Goals and incentives are at the heart
of any major corporate transformation. The incentives need to be logical,
fully aligned, and supportive of the overall goals of the transformation. This
is easy to get wrong; pricing leaders often find a lack of alignment not only
between the goals and the incentives of the sales force but also between the
goals of various organizational functions. All too frequently, misaligned incentives encourage reps to push lower-margin products or offer discounts
when they should stand firm. I have heard from many sales professionals in
organizations who end up confused about the company's priority, such as
a supervisor who wants volume to make the top line numbers at the same
time as the C-suite pushes for bigger profits. Many of these sales professionals have expressed their frustration with the lack of goal alignment. Unre-
solved, this frustration can result in disengagement and lack of motivation.
In addition, not all incentives are equally useful; surprise incentives can
have a tremendous impact in encouraging teams to go the extra mile.

Motivation tends to depend on getting a number of large and small
incentives right. Managers should take care to balance the ratio of personal
versus team-based rewards in order to promote both individual and collective confidence. Table 7.3 describes specific actions that leaders can use to
boost the motivation of individuals and teams to win their support in the
overall pricing transformation project.

3. Experiment

As discussed in the capabilities and change chapters of the book, experimentation is a core part of any change-management process. Experiments allow
people to try new methodologies and new concepts without being intimidated by the scope of the project and without fearing a failure that would
put them at personal risk. Successful experiments such as those shown in
Table 7.4 can be used to create a positive buzz in the organization. They also
help generate internal support for future and larger-scale projects. But most
of all, these initial test projects can serve as experiments to measure the

Table 7.3 Specific actions for the motivation dimension

Programs	Specific actions
Goal alignment	Align goal systems with overall corporate goals. Align goal systems with the goals of the pricing transformation. Develop a cascade of goals to ensure alignment at all levels. Communicate goal alignment through top and middle management to get buy-in.
Value-based incentives	Design a road map to transition incentive systems to a balanced volume/value portfolio. Align the timing of the incentives redesign with thresholds of the pricing transformation. Make initial changes in incentives at the top to encourage managers to lead by example. Include specific and relevant pricing metrics in the overall compensation plan. Include special qualitative incentives based on adoption of value programs.
Personal spot rewards	Create branded personal monetary spot awards. Allocate awards and rewards to various components of the pricing transformation. Set aside particular portions of personal rewards to be distributed by top executives.
Team-based rewards	Create branded team awards and rewards. Focus on team lunches and team events to avoid award distribution issues. Create friendly competition among teams to generate a boost in competitive spirit.

impact of pricing. Pricing practitioners often lack the knowledge and tools to measure the overall return on investment of pricing. However, with help from members of their pricing council, they can measure and document success to promote pricing up, down, and sideways in the organization. A successful project gives pricing professionals the raw material for success stories, best-practices sheets, and storylines they can use internally to boost confidence in the overall capacity of the organization, giving them the confidence to take on large pricing projects.

Many firms that have been in the midst of a transformation in pricing also report that quick wins can tremendously boost the level of team confidence and participation. Recently, a company that presented at a pricing software conference reported that an early quick win generated $300,000 in incremental profit very early on the pricing software deployment process.

Table 7.4 Specific actions for the experimentation dimension

Programs	Specific actions
Pilot programs	Design small-scale pilot programs to demonstrate the feasibility of pricing projects. Invite multiple functions to take part in pilot projects. Design and run multiple small pilot projects in parallel that are managed in the pricing council. Carefully select the members of the pilot team to ensure pilot project success. Measure and report pilot project success across the organization.
Case studies	Invite pricing champions to develop and present their case/success stories. Create a corporate template for all case studies and success stories. Document case studies with the approval of customers and partners. Use case studies internally during training and externally as a weapon during negotiations. Post authorized positive case/success stories on websites and blogs.
Best practices	Document lessons learned and best practices to share internally. Update training manuals to reflect key findings of internal pricing projects. Share best practices through SharePoint or on the corporate intranet. Create webinars for key stakeholders in the organization. Capture early all knowledge, processes, and documents created during projects.
Role-playing and shadowing	Include role-playing as part of the transformative training program. Conduct role-playing during sales force negotiation training. Encourage all staff members to participate in role-playing and shadowing programs. Hire value coaches to travel with the sales force for reinforcement and coaching. Encourage new hires to shadow pricing champions for a few weeks.

That news got the attention of the CEO and was widely celebrated, giving the pricing team a huge boost of momentum.

4. Transform

One thing I have learned in the pricing transformations I have conducted is that it's not just about convincing the sales team. You need to encourage all the functions to work together—even human resources. Human resources officers are often seen as nonstrategic to pricing projects. However, their cooperation is crucial. Role redefinitions, changes in job descriptions, modifications of incentive plans, internal communications plans, and the integration of the pricing projects in the overall performance management system all involve HR-controlled functions. In my view, a pricing transformation cannot be done without the deep-seated support of HR (Table 7.5).

If HR won't get involved, sales and marketing organizations can set up formal coaching or shadowing programs. One quick way to get started is to

Table 7.5 Specific actions for the transformation dimension

Programs	Specific actions
Training programs	Create a road map of training programs that will be deployed in the organization.
	Adopt a modular approach to training and make sure all functions receive relevant training.
	Identify qualified internal trainers and external credible experts to deliver training.
	Design a train-the-trainer approach to transfer and diffuse all necessary knowledge.
	Use technology to avoid disrupting the day-to-day business operation.
	Make sure middle managers receive all relevant training.
Coaching programs	Develop robust coaching programs for any employee requiring change reinforcement.
	Embed value coaches with the sales force to do field coaching and negotiation shadowing.
	Tie coaching activities to individual performance improvement plans.
	Consider hiring a corporate transformational coach to support top leadership.
Performance management plan	Modify performance documents for all relevant stakeholders to align goals and objectives.
	Include key parts of the pricing transformation in performance review discussions.
	Design appropriate performance improvement plans and a process to manage noncompliance.
	Be prepared to fire particularly recalcitrant employees.
	Develop new sets of recruitment guidelines that include key competencies
Language modification programs	Develop a list of key terms and expressions to be distributed widely.
	On occasion, measure the nature of words used during meetings: *value, change, positive*, etc.
	Develop a pricing objection management guide that includes value messages.
	Offer presentation and language training to the entire staff.

set up an informal buddy system for professionals who are struggling with pricing. In other words, you pair champions with people who struggle and let them work together. That creates solidarity and boosts collective confidence at the team level.

5. Convince

Price increases are typically "thrown over the wall" to sales teams without any explanation. Because the teams don't understand their rationale, they tend to have a hard time making the new price stick. Many sales professionals refer to pricing teams as the "No Department" whose decisions come out of a black box. This perception needs to be tackled head on! Instead of just telling them, show them the scientific process that went into setting the price. Sharing the science, the data, and the analysis that led to the new price schedule can help commercial staff (and other stakeholders) understand that the decisions were not made out of thin air or based on gut feelings. Making the price-setting process transparent can help the sales team in particular feel more confident about the price and better able to convince customers of its fairness. Specific activities to convince them are listed in Table 7.6.

6. Communicate

Pricing leaders tend to grossly underestimate the value of communication in any transformational program. Communication is essential to keep everyone on the same page. You should communicate progress to reinforce the project's branding, goals, and vision. One way to speed acceptance is to build an internal brand for the transformation project with a jazzy name, a logo, a slogan or tagline, and templates that can be used across the board. The cost of doing this is minimal, but the impact on the perceived professionalism of the initiative may be priceless. Project branding is especially relevant during the phase of change reinforcement when messages have to be repeated over and over. Other key communications measures are listed in Table 7.7.

Communication also means regular touch points among groups of professionals who are in the midst of deployment. For example, weekly sales calls can be set up to discuss progress with pricing actions, to share success

Table 7.6 Specific actions for the rationality dimension

Programs	Specific actions
Price decision rationale	Explain the rationale of all major price decisions affecting the commercial process.
	Encourage commercial functions to participate in the pricing council.
	Conduct training for all relevant commercial functions by showing case studies.
	Provide a price decision rationale that can be used by the sales force in front of customers.
Scientific tools and models	Train all commercial teams on the basics of pricing and pricing process methodologies.
	Develop simple models and simulators to show the power of sensitivity analysis.
	Equip the sales force with simple margin calculators or dollarization tools.
	Provide commercial teams with a nontechnical description of all pricing science being used.
Team-based decision making	Involve all relevant stakeholders in pilot projects and significant pricing decisions.
	Establish the pricing council as the central body to make team decisions.
	Create multifunctional teams to engage in strategic pricing programs.
	Design a process to ensure that no pricing decision is made without validation by relevant stakeholders.
Dynamic pricing-management systems	Train your staff to understand the basic principles of your dynamic pricing system.
	Explain in plain English the critical drivers and levers of your dynamic pricing models.
	Train all relevant stakeholders on the foundation of dynamic pricing.

stories, to anticipate customer reactions, and to troubleshoot difficult situations. Many of the firms I interviewed for my research conduct these calls. One even records success stories to capture the emotional charge of their sales reps as they describe a pricing win!

Most firms will think of a few of these programs but neglect others. Obviously, every firm faces budget and resource limitations, but I cannot stress enough that the more of these measures you pursue, the better your chance of a successful transformation. Do these programs work? Yes, they work—I have even witnessed them working too well. One of the companies I spent quite a bit of time with had turned their commercial teams into what they

Table 7.7 Specific actions for the communication dimension

Programs	Specific actions
Internal promotion of pricing programs	Create a formal branding strategy for the pricing transformation project. Use all branding materials for communication purposes and in training sessions. Create a dedicated intranet page, blog, or SharePoint site on the transformation project.
Pricing in corporate communication	Encourage the corporate communications team to include the project name and logo in corporate programs. Include transformational project parameters and success stories in the annual report. Mention the pricing project in corporate town hall meeting and videos.
Communication from the C-suite	Stay close to key executive assistants to get access to executive sponsors and the C-suite schedule. Provide a regular project update to the C-suite using a simple one-page traffic-light visual to show progress. Communicate quarterly pricing wins to the C-suite directly and ask for support in celebrating them. Invite executive sponsors and C-suite members to all formal and significant sessions.
Holistic and systematic messaging	Prepare a holistic communication plan that can be used throughout the years of the journey. Invest significant time and thought in designing the branding of the project. Enroll your organization's communications teams for both internal and external support.

called "price warriors." Leadership began to worry that they had created a monster and that their reps' confidence might turn to arrogance—and you absolutely don't want arrogance.

Pricing Confidence Versus Pricing Arrogance

As I mentioned earlier, over the past few years I've come to realize that confidence is the fuel that powers the engine of change. Confidence gives organizations the power to undertake the sustained and massive effort they need to make a significant change, such as a pricing transformation. But instilling confidence is not the same as training people to be arrogant; value-based pricing works only if it is truly value-based. In my research, I found that the only way an organization is able to charge a premium price is when that price is justified by the value of the product. Value-based pricing isn't gouging—gouging is easy, but not sustainable—it's about understanding what the customer values and then charging what it takes to deliver that value consistently and over the long haul.

Sometimes, success leads companies to overshoot their proper level of pricing confidence. I have seen several companies that have had to deal with pricing arrogance. This sometimes happens once the sales force succeeds in establishing some new prices. One of the organizations I studied at length implemented twelve significant price increases over 18 months, a heady experience that threatened to turn the sales reps into bullies that customers would flee from the minute they found a substitute vendor.

There is a fine line between confidence and arrogance, particularly when it comes to pricing (Liozu 2011). Leaders should pay close attention when a company has a unique market position and high pricing power. They need to instill a sense of respect and mindfulness in their reps when they inform customers of a new pricing structure. Value-based pricing must be seen as fair by both sides for the arrangement to endure. If the new price doesn't create value for everyone, the customer will eventually take his business elsewhere.

Conclusion: Only Believe

One of the most important factors in any kind of education is belief—belief in yourself, belief that what you are learning is worth learning, and belief that your teachers know what they're doing. A pricing transformation is no different. You can accomplish some without it, but the more you believe in yourself, your subject, and your instructors, the better. Psychologists will tell you that simply feeling that you are equal to the challenge begins to make you more equal to the challenge.

The good news, however, as sports psychologist Saul Miller has noted, is that team confidence has two components: memories of past successes and the preparation behind those successes. The less success the team has had, the greater the role preparation must play. In his book *Why Teams Win*, Miller quotes Roger Staubach, the Hall of Fame quarterback turned real estate developer, as saying, "The most important thing is preparation. . . . It takes a lot of unspectacular preparation to get spectacular results" (Miller 2009:97). Organizational confidence in pricing is no different.

Confidence: Some Tips to Get Started

1. As part of the pricing capabilities assessment, evaluate your sales force readiness for change and willingness to learn new things. Conduct a similar analysis for marketing, innovation, customer service, and technical support teams.

2. Conduct a confidence survey with the sales force early on to gauge the level of resistance you might face.

3. Design intentional confidence programs using the value-capture confidence revolution tool. Start first with the easy programs and slowly expand to other functions and to more advanced programs.

4. Set up meetings with your human resources department to bring them up to speed on the organizational confidence concept and to design the initial programs from the get-go.

5. Set up a meeting with the sales leaders to discuss the potential confidence breakdowns in the sales force and introduce the value-capture confidence revolution tool and programs.

Note

1. This notion of effort is also supported by other authors. Confidence consists of "positive expectations" for favorable outcomes and tremendous potential results (Hoover and Valenti 2005:244). It influences the individual member's willingness to invest in money, reputation, and emotional energy to shape the ability to perform (Kanter 2006:7).

In this chapter, I use the terms *organizational efficacy* and *organizational confidence* interchangeably and adopt Bohn's definition and properties of organizational confidence as organizational factors affecting the adoption-of-pricing approach:

> Organizational efficacy is a generative capacity within an organization to cope effectively with the demands, challenges, stressors and opportunities it encounters within the business environment. It exists as an aggregated judgment of an organization's individual members about their (1) sense of collective capacities, (2) sense of mission or purpose, and (3) a sense of resilience. In its most basic form, organizational efficacy is a sense of "can do." (Bohn 2001, 2002)

8 Possible Roadblocks Along the Journey

Change is a campaign, not a decision. CEOs can demand, but the people must want to act. Visions must be sold over & over.

Rosabeth Moss Kanter, Twitter

What have we learned so far? The pricing journey is a long one. To prepare for it, pricing professionals need to draw up a detailed road map and pay close attention to the 5 Cs of pricing transformation. But even detailed planning is no guarantee of success. The journey to value-based and disciplined pricing is also complex, and a lot can go wrong before your transformation is achieved (Dolan 1995). Actually, that is putting it too optimistically; I can guarantee that a lot *will* go wrong. Organizations being what they are, and people being what they are, sooner or later you will face a serious obstacle (Hinterhuber and Liozu 2012). If in addition to pricing-related problems you consider the sheer number of changes in market dynamics, regulation, and leadership that buffet any large enterprise in a given four-to-seven-year stretch, you'll realize that your chances of an entirely smooth rollout are almost nil.

Based on my experience in conducting and leading pricing transformations, and with the input of many other pricing professionals, I have identified the twelve most common organizational roadblocks companies meet on their pricing journey (Table 8.1). You won't be able to avoid all of them, but I hope that simply knowing what to expect will make it easier to cope with these situations when they arise.

1. Facing Lack of Courage and Will in the C-Suite

Challenge. Conducting a large-scale organizational and cultural transformation requires a steady, long-term commitment from top management

Table 8.1 List of potential roadblocks

1. Facing lack of courage and will in the C-suite
2. Giving up when it gets too hard
3. Overfocusing on analytical capabilities
4. Taking a unidimensional view of pricing
5. Rushing the journey
6. Succumbing to market turbulences and commoditization
7. Misrepresenting the scope of the transformational process
8. Not addressing the root causes of pricing problems
9. Underestimating the complexity of pricing and of the change agenda
10. Underestimating the difficulty of converting the sales force
11. Failing to introduce value-based pricing into the core business
12. Facing uncontrollable events that derail the transformation

(Liozu et al. 2012). Courage is needed when market pressures increase, when the organization is stuck in old paradigms, or when the shareholders request immediate results. Courage is needed as well to stay the course with the team, to stick to the value strategy, and to be ready to take a step back before jumping two steps ahead. If a pricing initiative is to succeed, company leaders can't "go wobbly," as Margaret Thatcher used to say; they must risk their time, their reputation, and their political capital to push forward despite a real risk of failure. And if your company has a politically charged culture, the C-suite will need to be prepared to keep supporting the transformation even after initial enthusiasm wanes, a breakdown occurs, or a failure is exposed.

A pricing transformation also often requires executives to learn a new kind of expertise, and it's tough to teach top dogs new tricks. Although most executives will have heard the pitch about the value of the transformation, and may even nod enthusiastically when it is proposed, in practice, they will resist orders to learn an entirely new discipline. Naturally enough, many executives end up going to some lengths to avoid the kind of ego-bruising work such a radical change entails. They become unable to listen to the information they need to hear before they can lead the charge, or find reasons to avoid learning something new that is pricing related. A few of these leaders may delegate the entire project to a senior manager and decide not to get involved at all.

Top-level disengagement typically leaves a power vacuum that allows other managerial problems to develop. Middle management may not support a program that they don't see yielding much benefit to their unit or themselves. Organizational confidence may dissipate and lead to a shift of resources and attention to other products. With little attention at the top focused on the transformation, tensions, conflicts, and power struggles may arise that slow or derail the pricing agenda—particularly if resources are cut off before the transformation is complete.

Solution. Leaders are human, just like everybody else—sometimes more so. History is full of examples of individuals whose extraordinary leadership abilities were counterbalanced by unusually grave character flaws. Two measures may encourage leaders to stay the course: first, to extract a promise that the C-suite will devote a certain number of hours per month to pricing-related issues, and second, to align compensation policies with pricing incentives. Creating strategic alignment from the C-suite to the front lines is the best way to generate momentum and buy-in across the organization. One executive cannot do it all. You will need to bring several top leaders to the pricing council so that middle management understands that the pricing transformation is a critical priority for the organization. Finally, make sure you diffuse knowledge in multiple directions—downward, sideways, and upward. Top leaders need to learn about value and pricing management even more than people further down the ladder. Make sure knowledge flows freely in the organization.

2. Giving Up When It Gets Too Hard

Challenge. During Stages 1 and 2 of the transformational model presented in Chapter 2 of the book, the going often gets rough. Sometimes, the situation may even become chaotic. Many organizations embark on a pricing transformation only to uncover all kinds of things they were happier not knowing about—outdated systems, bad data, dysfunctional pricing levels, and nonexistent price discipline. Like a home remodeling project that leads you to find termites in the floor, this discovery won't necessarily make the pricing team more popular even though the termites aren't your fault. Top leaders may look at this mess and decide to stop searching before more bad news is uncovered. Other stakeholders may reject the project from the get-go because it exposes their inefficient and potentially destructive actions from the past. I once discussed this situation with a pricing executive who told me that after discovering bad internal data, he and his team had to spend 18 months cleaning up the mess before continuing their transformational work. The discovery of the bad data dissipated the team's momentum. They lost all credibility with the executive suite. In the presence of these kinds of difficulties, leaders often decide to stop or postpone projects—or find an excuse to kill the messenger.

Solution. Conduct a thorough pricing capabilities assessment that will identify the most significant gaps and priorities to work on during the early stages of the transformation. Make sure the result of the pricing capabilities assessment is not communicated widely, especially if serious issues need to be addressed. Focus on building a strong foundation in pricing even if you have to delay the next stages of the transformation. The stages of discovery and exploration are the ideal times to build a strong foundation that will enable the company to build its pricing system properly and with assurance. Finally, conduct this early discovery process with a mindful approach. Make it clear to the team that all firms have dysfunctionalities in pricing and that the team focus should be on moving forward, not dwelling on the past.

3. Overfocusing on Analytical Capabilities

Challenge. Many firms embark on pricing transformation programs thinking that advanced pricing is something they can buy. They install the software but forget to allot time and money to train the people who are supposed to operate it. Often, these same firms delegate the change-management activities the new system demands to project managers who have not received any formal change-management training. This inevitably slows down overall adoption of new pricing tools, builds resistance to the program, and can leave the organization in a worse situation than before it began. Focusing too much on analytical capabilities and the system dimension of pricing often leads the company to lose sight of its larger goal.

Solution. Invest in your people as well as your hardware. Training and expertise almost always pay off when integrating a complex new system into the organization. As the bumper sticker says, if you think education is expensive, try ignorance. To make sure you aren't being misled about usage, measure not only your overall adoption but also your usage rate. If the new systems are not being used, find out why and develop training programs that can build confidence. Make sure the change road map you design up front doesn't overlook the importance of user adoption, user interpretation of data, and the human side of analytics.

4. Taking a Unidimensional View of Pricing

Challenge. Pricing is not unidimensional. Multiple agents are involved in pricing and pricing activities that may be internal versus external, cost-based versus value-based, user-based versus industry-based, and rational versus emotional (Liozu 2012). Considering pricing as a unidimensional function encourages reductionist behaviors and oversimplifications (Liozu, Hinterhuber, Perelli, et al. 2012). For example, setting prices solely on costs ignores the other two Cs of price setting (customer and competition) that affect a price.

Solution. *Map out the various stakeholders and critical components of your pricing ecosystem. Ensure that your pricing strategies include all critical dimensions, not only customers, costs, and competition but also trade channels, buyers, and other stakeholders, as shown in Figure 8.1. This is best achieved by forming multifunctional teams that work together to deploy pricing resources*

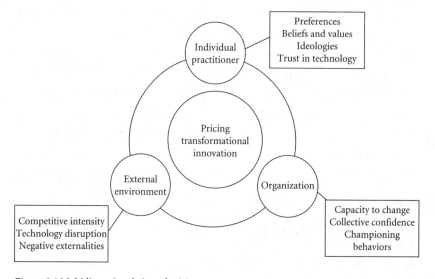

Figure 8.1 Multidimensional view of pricing

and execute pricing activities. With a strong accountability culture, the various stakeholders will help each other achieve greater results.

5. Rushing the Journey

Challenge. In an environment where no one thinks more than one fiscal quarter ahead, few managers have ever had the experience of leading a four-to-seven-year change-management program. People are often tempted to try to accelerate the process, but my research suggests that slow and steady really does win the race when it comes to pricing; nearly 70 percent of corporate transformations fail, often because of a greed for speed. A pricing transformation requires significant up-front investment, sweat equity, and executive attention before any payback is achieved. There may be some quick wins along the way, but in my experience it takes at least 18 to 24 months to start seeing some credible and tangible results. It's not easy to get the pace right. Go too fast and employees will become overwhelmed and start resisting the new processes. Go too slow and you won't be able to create enough momentum to sustain the reform.

Solution. The successful completion of internal milestones should be celebrated, but they need to be kept far enough apart that the organization has time to digest the changes and accept them as a new normal. Rewards should be given for thoroughness, not speed. Explain the need for paced change to top executives. They will be sensitive to the value of incremental investments and should appreciate—at least initially—that more control can be achieved in a slow-paced change-management process. Show them a road map that includes thresholds and milestones of user adoption and usage rates, and stick to those thresholds. Finally, test the level of absorption of knowledge and concepts by gauging the sophistication of pricing discussions and pricing projects. Only after the knowledge sticks will the company be ready to proceed to the next stage of the transformation. Finally, as with any improvement project, leverage the quick wins you may discover early on to buy time with anxious, time-pressured executives. If your organization requires quick results, you may have to design a different road map that focuses on both short-term wins and long-term transformational success.

6. Succumbing to Market Turbulences and Commoditization

Challenge. Competitive intensity, market disruptions, and environmental turbulence can slow down the adoption and implementation of change initiatives. Because the customer-value assessment process requires the identification and evaluation of factors that differentiate a firm's products from those of the competition (Hinterhuber 2004; Nagle and Holden 2002), any changes in the competitors' product value proposition may impact the firm's position on the customer value map (Smith and Nagle 2005).

In addition, changes in environmental dynamics may generate a collective inability to predict and adjust to the environment. Managers can become overwhelmed by the amount of competitive information and the number of pricing decisions they have to make (Dutta, Zbaracki, and Bergen 2003). A high level of risk and turbulence in a market requires quick reflexes and a strong capability to respond in a timely manner. Increases in competitive activities, such as an accelerated rate of obsolescence, can generate more stress, uncertainty, and "unanalyzability" of market information (Daft and Weick 1984). This may in turn lead to a reduction in the company's ability to buffer against uncertainties (Lynn 2005) and its ability to change (Judge and Douglas 2009).

Fierce competition can make it more difficult to pursue a value-based pricing strategy as well. One study of 78 industrial companies in Belgium found that in situations of increased competitive intensity, companies tend to lean more toward cost-based pricing strategies (Ingenbleek et al. 2001). When markets are depressed and multiple suppliers are offering relatively undifferentiated products, discounting and price wars start to occur and can lead to ineffective pricing behaviors (Shipley and Bourdon 1990). If the industry's products begin to be treated as commodities, buyers may find themselves locked in traditional pricing patterns and routines based on competitive references. As industries mature, they will experience more aligned and homogeneous pricing practices due to declining demand and increased competition (Shipley and Bourdon 1990). This may lead buyers to rely on a smaller group of key vendors, increasing the pricing pressure and leading perhaps to unwanted transparency in the industry's value models.

Solution. Focus on the customer. People almost always overestimate price sensitivity. Even in the case of the best-known price around, the price of gas, some gas stations realized long ago that simply adding amenities such as safe and attractive bathrooms could reduce price sensitivity. The stations couldn't charge an extra dollar a gallon for that service, but the market would tolerate a few pennies, and even a few pennies more had a dramatic impact on profitability. If you can find anything that the customer wants that the other providers have not offered—a B2B supplier, for instance, may offer an original equipment manufacturer (OEM), a more convenient schedule, or more complete component—you can become a premium provider. By working on all three critical dimensions of price setting (cost, competition, and customers), you can modulate the attention paid to each of them during times of competitive pressure. The key is to keep focusing on customer value even in periods when you are faced with tough competition or a cost squeeze.

7. Misrepresenting the Scope of the Transformational Process

Challenge. Many pricing projects stall or derail because the up-front expectations did not materialize. The plan wasn't thought through very well; the case studies used to sell and guide a transformation didn't turn out to have much to do with what the company needs to accomplish; the external benchmarks they use don't fit the company's situation. Benchmarks encourage imitation (Pfeffer and Sutton 2006) and "copy and paste" behaviors (DiMaggio and Powell 1983) that can be detrimental to the accuracy of the project cost evaluation. A lack of quantitative data on the ROI of pricing also makes it more difficult for analytical executives to "keep the faith."

Solution. Stick to the facts. Stage 2 is the solution-seeking period, when pricing leaders begin to shape potential solutions to the pricing issues. It's easy to overpromise. Begin instead with a sober pricing capabilities assessment, which will list all major issues and gaps facing the organization's pricing. That process, combined with an external benchmark, can make for a powerful road map. It's also important to design the program in a way that never underplays the costs, the difficulty, or the long-term nature of the project. However, that is not to say you won't need to sell the program and keep on selling it. After all, hopelessness is an impossible sale. The transformation must be designed instead in such a way as to show consistent progress, through the example of pilot programs (particularly for innovative products that don't touch the core business), and against key pricing-related KPIs.

8. Not Addressing the Root Causes of Pricing Problems

Challenge. Many companies hire pricing consultants to address their price erosion problems or to reduce the complexity of their pricing process. These companies clearly state that the time has come to address their "pricing problems" and stop the bad discounting behaviors. Hiring a consultant provides leaders with a temporary sense of relief that the situation will improve in the short to medium term. Unfortunately, pricing problems are often just symptoms of deeper internal problems related to the business model or corporate strategy (Figure 8.2).

If these root causes are not clearly addressed at some point in the transformation, the symptoms will not go away and the firm will be stuck in the Zone of Good Intentions described in the Pricing Capability Grid shown in Chapter 2.

Solution. *Don't overlook the importance of conducting business strategy and business model reviews before you launch the pricing transformation. Pricing leaders should flag the root causes of their pricing problems and make sure top business leaders understand the implications. Structural issues need to be addressed prior to devoting resources and attention to pricing problems.*

Figure 8.2 Not addressing the root cause of pricing problems

The most common problems include a lack of segmentation, a lack of strategic alignment, or an obsolete corporate business strategy. Encourage business leaders to explore the root cause of some of the pricing symptoms during the existing strategic planning process. Guide marketing managers to pay close attention to segmentation analysis. If your company hires a pricing consulting firm to fix your pricing issues, you may run into difficulties in addressing these issues. Defining the scope early on with them may be a bit challenging until you discover what is really preventing pricing symptoms from being addressed.

9. Underestimating the Complexity of Pricing and of the Change Agenda

Challenge. The sheer difficulty of managing a pricing revolution is frequently underestimated. Unlike many technical initiatives where the CEO can simply tell the CTO to "make it so," the multiple changes required to convert the organization to value-based pricing demand an effort at every level of the organization.

Underestimating the complexity of pricing can lead to serious mistakes, particularly if it leads you to making changes in a dynamic system (Figure 8.3). Many companies do not adequately prepare their sales force and

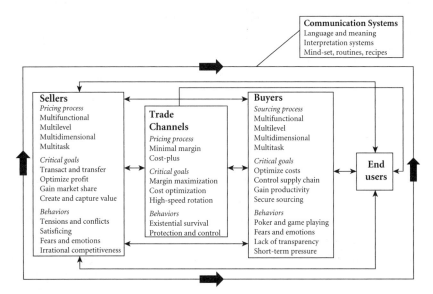

Figure 8.3 Misunderstanding pricing complexity

marketing staff to face market resistance after the launch of a new pricing strategy. Without careful preparation, customer-facing staff can become embittered and long-time customers alienated from the organization if they feel the price changes are made in a high-handed way that does not seem justified.

Solution. *Make sure that no elements of the change are orphans, especially if you are facing a complex value chain structure with lots of moving parts. Every aspect needs to be led by a specific senior executive. These leaders should map out pockets of resistance and work to convert them in advance. Project managers are often ill-equipped to cope with change management. If you are a pricing professional, obtain your change-management certification before you begin the pricing initiative. You will need to become a change agent to manage this level of complexity and to help all your relevant stakeholders cope with the changes the pricing transformation will entail.*

10. Underestimating the Difficulty of Converting the Sales Force

Challenge. Most companies forget to bring the sales force into the pricing transformation. Often, management drops new pricing methods, systems, and tools in their lap and expects instant adoption. This is an expensive mistake; Deloitte Research reports that over 50 percent of the impact of pricing comes from the execution side. If your sales force is not on board with your pricing initiatives, chances are your entire pricing transformation will not go well. In fact, that 50 percent will be half of zero without the support of sales. In my experience, you simply cannot achieve a pricing transformation without the support, buy-in, and total collaboration of the sales force.

The highest levels of resistance will come from the commercial midmanagement group. They generally dictate the priorities of the sales teams. Because they prospered under the old rules of the game, convincing them that those old rules were a mistake can be a huge challenge. They tend to be the hardest people to convince of the wisdom of this new way of working and of being compensated, but you need them. Without the full support of the sales organization, the credibility of your pricing data will be challenged; customer information will not circulate freely; spanners will be thrown into the works of the pilot project; and other projects will start popping up in the queue ahead of yours. A dozen moves into the game and you'll already be checkmated.

Solution. *Get sales on board as soon as possible. Sales leaders should be involved in the design of every pricing process, method, and tool to encourage their early buy-in. Persuade sales leaders to take charge of some pricing initiatives and involve representatives of the sales force in multifunctional team meetings. Although even this may not be enough, such an effort will certainly improve your chance of success and may accelerate the deployment of pricing programs. Finally, never doubt that as difficult as the change is, the transformation is ultimately the right thing for your company and your customers— and getting it right before your competitors do is crucial. As marketing guru Seth Godin says, "Change almost never fails because it's too early. It almost always fails because it's too late."*

11. Failing to Introduce Value-Based Pricing Into the Core Business

Challenge. Particularly in hard times, cautious executives often hold themselves back from introducing value-based pricing where it might actually matter: the core business.

Through the long, hard years of our ongoing economic crisis, I have come to realize that deploying value-based pricing in the core business of an organization is a challenging proposition. Few people want to rock the boat even in the best of times, and they're even less eager to want to make changes when they're coping with 20-foot swells and the engine is making a funny noise. In my discussions with pricing practitioners whose transformational projects stalled or sank, I found a number of factors that stopped their leaders from focusing on the larger goal:

Cost is the priority. In times of crisis, business leaders often put more emphasis on cost management and operational excellence in the core business. With tight budgets and constrained resources, they may be reluctant to launch something as complex as a value-based pricing project. They are likely to feel particularly risk averse as well and doubtful about a plan that could require introducing products at a higher price with potential implications on volume and market share.

Leaders are reluctant to change. Deploying value-based pricing in an entire core business requires a lot of changes in the selling process. Changing during times of uncertainty can accentuate the potential trauma associated with changes in roles and responsibilities.

Commoditization of the core business is rising. Many firms have lost differentiation in their core business and are struggling to justify price premiums. This long crisis has eroded business models and customers' willingness to pay. Competitive pressure reinforces the use of formula-based pricing approaches (Ingenbleek 2007).

Leaders are focused entirely on market share. I have spoken with many executives who have taken a defensive position to retain market share in hopes of a return to higher demand in the near future. With attention focused on volume and market share optimization, leaders are not willing to walk away from deals and volume opportunities—and that makes a value-based pricing discussion difficult, to say the least.

Solution. *If your company is going through a rough period, hold back on a big-bang deployment of value-based pricing even if it further delays your transformation. A better approach is usually to inject the value story at multiple entry points that are not at the core of the organization. I propose a disruptive approach to getting started with the journey that involves identifying the potential "cracks" in the core business and injecting value through these cracks. Progressive infiltration of value-based pricing can be done in five ways:*

Segmentation. *Most companies regularly revisit their segmentation strategies and validate the robustness of their customer segments. In doing so, they also open the door to a potential modification of the marketing strategy for each segment, including the pricing strategy. Pricing professionals should be aware of these exercises and make sure they participate in the overall process.*

Price changes. *Another opportunity to inject value-based pricing knowledge into the core business is during the preparation and execution of price changes. When price increases are prepared, products with greater pricing power are typically considered for higher price increases. Most firms base their price increases on cost increases they received from suppliers, dooming them forever to limited profitability. During these discussions, pricing professionals can introduce the concepts of value maps and value models and try to persuade them that it is better to base their price increases on their offering's value than their delivery costs. The customer value quantification or dollarization method can be a good way to show differentiation value as competitors change their prices. This is an excellent opportunity to introduce value-based pricing tools into the price change-management process. Once you've used it, you've opened the door for further price-level discussions of targeted offerings in each segment.*

New-product development. *This is probably the most powerful point of infiltration for value-based pricing. Innovation and pricing teams should work closely to extract more value from innovative products, particularly if they are following an economic value estimation process analysis. Each new-product opportunity should be evaluated based on net differentiation value and assigned a price based on customer value. The customer research necessary to support this exercise can be done in conjunction with the innovation team. The goal is to make sure that each new product entering the core business does so with the right price based on the customer's perceived value and estimated willingness to pay. Slowly, over the course of a few years, the core business will begin to integrate right-priced products.*

Service innovation. *The same methods can be used for service innovation. If your product offerings are somewhat commoditized, introducing additional valuable services may be the answer—but only assuming the innovative new services are not given away for free. Value-based pricing can help the company assess the value of these services and create price menus for various levels of service performance. The critical step is to find a way to estimate the value of services and to use them to justify price premiums.*

Introducing new offerings. *One size does not fit all. As part of category management, various performance/price profiles may be introduced to the market in response to specific customer needs. Any new version in a specific product or service line is an opportunity to set the price based on customer-perceived value and not cost. In that case, pricing professionals can help analyze the trade-offs between performance and price by running a conjoint analysis. They can also support product management with the pricing strategy for the whole category by injecting more voice-of-customer research.*

Success in value-based pricing comes down to determination. Even if, in an anxious time, a full-scale transformation seems out of reach, value-based pricing advocates can usually find ways to begin working toward a transformation. This may not lead to a victory in the short run, but somewhere down the line, after some of these experiments start to succeed, someone will eventually ask, why is this product line so much more profitable than our others?

12. Facing Uncontrollable Events That Derail the Transformation

Challenge. Many events can derail, slow down, or stop a pricing transformation process. A large acquisition or divestiture of business, a large-scale restructuring process, or an unexpected CEO change can all either stop the transformation or bring programs to a stop while the pricing advocates resell it all over again. This can be quite disruptive; I recently witnessed this at a large U.S.-based medical device company in which the new CEO did not believe in the centralized design for pricing and immediately dismantled the central pricing organization in charge of a transformation that was already well under way. After her axe fell, most of the pricing responsibilities and initiatives were decentralized to the business units, and the company's pricing transformation was set back by years.

Solution. *Prepare contingency plans for these types of unpredictable events. Document quick wins and constantly refresh the transformation business case so you are always prepared to justify the program's existence. There may be* *little you can do to prevent these abrupt changes, but you can soften the blow if you're ready for them.*

Conclusions

I am sure that by now that you get the point: a pricing transformation is not a walk in the park. It's an arduous and uncertain process that requires sweat equity and persistence. While it is worth the investment, be prepared to cope with many inevitable reversals: the twelve potential roadblocks I calculate are just the ones I see most frequently, but there are many more where that came from. My intention is not to scare you, but to prepare you for the challenge. A pricing transformation is a bit like a long-distance bicycle race: you can't avoid the pain, but you can prepare for it. As Tour de France winner Greg LeMond once said: "It never gets easier. You just go faster."

9 Pricing Myths at the Organizational Level

On your pricing journey, some of the worst roadblocks you will run into are obstacles that don't exist: the myths of pricing. These myths have existed for decades and have evolved over time. Still, a number are alive and kicking and will hurt your organization's ability to evolve if you don't root them out. They can't really stop you, but they do make it much harder for you to build the momentum your team needs to succeed.

Pricing is not unique in this respect. People are often held back not by reality but by their idea of reality—the kinds of misperceptions that poet William Blake described as "mind-forg'd manacles." Many companies have been destroyed, and even whole economies, because people clung to ideas that either had stopped working or had never worked. Pricing, however, is an area particularly susceptible to mythmaking, I think mostly because price setting is always very emotional. In addition, value-based price management is still a young methodology about which people are often ignorant, and gaps in knowledge tend to attract improvised explanations.

Over the past ten years, pricing experts have been more aggressive in talking about pricing myths, and many of the most outrageous have disappeared. Pricing executives' growing sophistication, the emergence of better pricing software, and the publication of a number of excellent books on pricing theory have all helped reduce the overall level of ignorance. Despite the work of the Professional Pricing Society and many first-rate pricing experts, however, many myths refuse to die. At the same time, a few new myths are popping up, generated mostly by people who don't understand the new theories.

Modern Pricing Myths

Last year, I asked my colleagues in the Professional Pricing Society LinkedIn group what myths they were running into most these days. Here are a few of the most insightful responses from among the dozens I collected:

Myth: "'To get started in pricing, you need huge resources.' This is a myth. If a firm does nothing in pricing, you can start paying attention without spending fortunes. I say, it takes courage and mindfulness to really get started."—CEO of a midsized manufacturing company

Myth: "'Pricing is not a creative function.' Au contraire again! Pricing is a dynamic science that requires adaptable strategies and tactics, creative problem solving and recommendations supporting changing environmental influences. Static pricing leads to erosion and loss of power. Innovation and creativity are key to pricing."—CEO of a midsized company

Myth: "The misconception that . . . the pricing team is the 'sales prevention department.'" To those that believe in this myth. . . . the reality is: pricers try to help capture sales opportunities, as well as maximize profits!"—Pricing practitioner with a long career in pricing management and consulting

Myth: "'That cost-based pricing is prudent and assures profitability.' In fact, cost-based pricing often fails to correctly characterize/allocate many costs; it assumes that costs can be passed on to the customer if they change; and it encourages a race to the bottom and commodification where the only winner will be the lowest-cost provider."—CEO of a value-based pricing software firm

Myth: "'Discounting is always bad and the result of poor sales discipline or poor initial pricing.' There are at least three good reasons to have a discounting strategy. (i) Establish a high reference price in the mind of the buyer (and leave room to give procurement the discounts they are expected to negotiate); (ii) to adjust price to value for specific customers; (iii) to invest in a target market or customer (as long as there is a clear path to getting a return on the investment)."—CEO of a pricing software company

Myth: "'I have to fix my price-delivery processes before I can improve my price-point quality.' This is like saying, 'I have to fix my plumbing leaks before I remove the lead in the water . . .' Nonsense—bad prices are toxic to your business and can/should be resolved right away. The profit lifts that come from fixing your price-point quality are a great source of funding for that eventual price-delivery project, by the way."—Director of pricing excellence at a pricing optimization software company

Myth: "'I can't put my prices up.' Why do I hear this so often when all around prices are rising? It's often an excuse for poor or weak leadership which results in cost cutting elsewhere to make up the difference."—Director of a commercial excellence consulting firm

Myth: "'The journey to price excellence starts with smart pricing systems (for analytics, execution and optimization).' This journey [actually] starts with understanding the markets and the customers."—Pricing thought leader

Myth: "'For achieving a better pricing performance, pricing authority has to be located within a centralized Pricing department instead of within Sales.'" The purpose of installing a (centralized) Pricing department is not to define single price points, but rather to manage and steer pricing processes!"—Pricing manager at an industrial group

Myth: "'This customer/this time is different, it's a special situation—we only need to discount this one time.' Word among customers does spread so it won't be just that customer asking for that discount. Also, in many B2B situations, the relationship between supplier and customer lasts for years. Next time they buy that product you will be asked to discount again—'just this once.'"—Managing director of a revenue management consulting company

Myth: "'What I am doing with spreadsheets and pricing databases is good enough.' Most companies I have encountered are not motivated to do anything because they think they already have their markets figured out as well as they can . . . concepts like value-based pricing, pricing optimization or improving price execution escape them. How many of us have spent hours convincing our prospects, customers, or internal teams that we can do pricing better than it is being done right now?"—Marketing executive in a pricing software optimization firm

Myth: "'Pricing & Conditions should be complex.' Au contraire! Pricing is all about making the complex simple. If your prices are not fair, transparent & easy to communicate, you don't have a pricing strategy. Pricing research must allow you to reduce complexity and gain in understanding of common behaviors. Same for sales policy and conditions: commercial levers should represent the variety of behavior but be simple to manipulate and incentivize the desired change in behavior."—Pricing expert and marketing professor (PhD)

Myth: "'To gain share we need to discount and sacrifice margins.' Fact: You can have higher than average margins and gain share as long as you can defend your price through the value you deliver to customers. You don't have to discount to gain share if you can truly differentiate your offerings in the market."—Director at a value-based pricing software company

Myth: "'The market became a commodity market'; 'The customer tells us the price'; 'we cannot increase our price.' Have you never heard these sentences? Of course, few customers wake up wanting to pay a higher price but most do seek value. It's the firm's responsibility to frame and deliver the value proposition and the pricing mechanism to capture this value."—Financial controller in charge of pricing for a large European service firm

And I keep collecting more. Just recently, I was delivering value modeling training to a multifunction group of managers in a large industrial company in Europe. One of the sales directors candidly asked me the following question at dinner at the end of the first day: "Do you really need a pricing team to manage pricing?" Of course you do! The myth that pricing can run itself while being fragmented is puzzling. I often respond to this one by asking, "Would you run your organization without a sales team?" Case closed.

The damage myths can do depends, of course, on the heads in which they are lodged. The most difficult to exorcise tend to be in the C-suite. Just recently again, while leading a pricing transformation for a midsized business in the eastern United States, I had to explain to a company's CEO and COO over and over why they needed to budget for change management. They were convinced that their one project manager could do the trick and that behaviors would change on their own. Unfortunately, that isn't the only company where, when it comes to pricing, the oxygen is a little thin at the top of the pyramid.

Myths at the Top of the Organization

Often, the myths at the top are as out of touch as they are fiercely held (as shown in Figure 9.1). Believe it or not, top executives will try to tell me that pricing is a tactical function and that they have no time to dedicate to it. In 2010, I had the pleasure of interviewing the CEO of a large chemical company. I asked him directly why he did not get involved in pricing. His response was as follows: *"With thirteen businesses, five thousand products, five thousand customers, it's absolutely impossible for me to be able to weigh in on pricing."* Obviously, I could not disagree more. A CEO cannot get involved in the nitty-gritty of pricing operations, but there are many ways to

Figure 9.1 Myths at the top

champion pricing at the strategic level. CEOs also often think that paying attention to margins is good enough. Out of the fifteen CEOs I interviewed during my qualitative inquiry process, most of those running businesses that used cost-based or competition-based pricing focused heavily on cost and margins. They did not seem to remember that margins are composed of volumes, cost of goods sold, and *prices*.

Myth: It Takes Millions to Get Started in Pricing

Managers always find reasons to put off thinking about pricing and justify their reluctance with whatever myth comes to mind. Most often, they complain about their lack of time and money and say that pricing is expensive, requires tremendous resources, and is useful only for large organizations. They could not be more wrong. As a matter of fact, I respectfully challenged a few top executives to list the number of costing analysts and purchasing analysts in their organization and then tell me how many pricing professionals they had. It was amazing to hear their responses; for example, after the CEO of an automotive component manufacturer told me he had six full-time employees working in the costing department, I asked him why he could not hire one person for pricing. His answer: too expensive. Of course, companies must watch costs too, but is the money coming in really just one sixth as important as the money going out?

Very often, firms and their leaders try to conduct a pricing transformation "on the cheap," without enough investment. Even before they launch the project, they immediately apply cost controls, thinking that one or two pricing professionals can transform the habits of 50 years and thousands of people. I recently visited a large petrochemical manufacturer with annual sales revenues of over $20 billion per year. They had just embarked on a pricing journey with three full-time marketing and pricing professionals. *Three.* How can you transform something that massive with a team of three?

Of course, you have to work with what you have. As shortsighted as most pricing professionals believe this approach to be, many teams will need to begin with a tiny budget. In Figure 9.2, I propose a number of ways to get started if they'll only give you a loaf and half a fish.

- Create a pricing council that meets every month to discuss price trends, competitive pressures, and new-product pricing. Invite your

Figure 9.2 How to get started

marketing, sales, and finance leaders and champion the process. Cash expense = $0.

· Buy several copies of the best pricing book you can find and give it to your key staff and members of the pricing council to read. Cash expense = $500.

· Send one or more of your marketing managers to a Professional Pricing Society conference. They will learn from the best, meet top pricing professionals, and gain lots of insights. Cash expense: $2,000.

· Take your best costing or financial analyst and give her the responsibility of applying the basic techniques picked up in the book and at the conference. Cash expense: $0.

· Join your local pricing network group, a group of pricing professionals who gather to network and share best practices. Cash expense: $250.

· Join all pricing groups on LinkedIn and leverage the expertise of online experts. Cash expense = $0.

· Register for free webinars from pricing experts or register for the PPS Core Pricing Skills online course. Cash expense = $500.

· Search for pricing documents online using Google Docs. There is a gold mine of information out there, from PowerPoint presentations to YouTube videos to case studies. Cash expense = $0.

Do all of those things and you will have spent a grand total of $3,250—and you will already be further down the road toward a pricing transformation than the average small- to midsized organization.

Keep it simple at the beginning. Do not overwhelm teams with heavy-duty analytics, but pursue some quick wins to build confidence. Establish basic processes and programs that get pricing activities off the ground. The cost of joining the pricing revolution is $3,250. But the value, as the Visa commercials say, is priceless!

Myth: Pricing Is a Purely Rational and Scientific Discipline

If pricing were pure science, our jobs would be easy. In fact, pricing is also an art. No pricing model is free of biases and incomplete assumptions, and as a result, no pricing decision is perfect. Pricing analysis requires maintaining a delicate balance between science-based decisions and intuition-based decisions. This can be a discouraging realization for people who start a pricing transformation with the idea that they are bringing their company's pricing into the light of reason. The truth is that as with most social science problems, there are only partially rational beings at either end of every transaction, which means that in even the most advanced pricing systems, intuition must still play a role. Scholars now agree that gut feelings have a legitimate role to play in decision making (Burke and Miller 1999), especially in situations of uncertainty or turbulence (Khatri and Ng 2000), novelty, or an HR problem. Experienced managers have learned a variety of schemas and patterns gained through experience and organized them "in terms of recognizable chunks and associated information" (Simon 1987). As Miller and Ireland (2005:21) suggest, paraphrasing Roy Rowan's work on the subject:

> Intuition is knowledge gained without rational thought. And since it comes from some stratum of awareness just below the conscious level, it is slippery and elusive, to say the least. New ideas spring from a mind that organizes experiences, facts, relationships to discern a mental path that has not been taken before.

When faced with a pricing decision or with the need to price a new product or service, pricing leaders do not have the luxury of choosing between an analytic approach and an intuitive approach. Managers need to be able to combine both approaches to reach a greater level of decision-making effectiveness (Dane and Pratt 2007; Simon 1987). The difference is that executives who are also pricing experts don't need to just "go with their gut"—they can take the data and reduce the level of uncertainty and ambiguity. Rather than make the entire pricing decision by intuition, they use their feelings to double-check the analysis, or to make an educated guess when faced with a new situation such as a new product or changing competitive dynamic.

Myth: Our Business Is a Commodity

Leaders in many companies complain about the commoditization of their products and services. They face extraordinary market conditions with aggressive competitive pressures and sophisticated commodity buyers. Sometimes—and this is worst of all—buyers categorize the company's offering as a commodity product and service and treat it more harshly than they do their suppliers whose offerings they consider premium and differentiated.

I feel for leaders of companies targeted this way—this isn't an easy situation—but I also have a habit of showing them some tough love after I've heard them use the word *commodity* themselves in the course of our discussions. It drives me nuts when I visit clients or partners and see the degree to which they are cutting themselves down without any help from the buyers. For instance, they often:

- Include the word *commodity* in the name of their business unit. If you include the word *commodity* in your name, naturally enough, customers will think you sell commodities. It also contaminates your service offerings and your corporate brand—not a very smart idea.

- Use the word *commodity* in their annual report and other publications: ditto. If you use the word *commodity* in your most important corporate communications, don't be surprised if people take you at your word.

- Include the word *commodity* in their daily vocabulary. This is also not very smart. The word *commodity* has connotations of a high-volume, low-price product. It conditions employees to see few opportunities for differentiation and no room for price improvement—and practically begs buyers to demand a price cut.

- Talk about commodities in their business and pricing strategies. Obviously, if you're talking about commodities all the time, chances are your business and pricing strategies will be commodity- or cost-based. If you surrender your pricing to market conditions, don't be surprised if you hear anything other than discount requests, tough price negotiations, and eroding margins.

·   Use the word *commodity* to excuse competitive pressure. Finally, based on these pricing strategies, the sales force will start using the word defensively. I am sure you have heard the following statement: "We are in a commodity business; I cannot do anything on price."

Repeat the word often enough, and the situation will come true: your offering will be turned into a commodity. *Attention, Kmart shoppers.* The buyers you are facing know that—and they will take advantage of it. Your employees will also start to act more like they work for a commodity provider—and their attitudes will follow. Worst of all, your salespeople will lose all confidence in your company's pricing. Any chance they have to push their margin won't be realized.

My view is straightforward. There is no such thing as a commodity. If you have customers today, you already have some kind of differentiation. You may not understand it, but it's there—the buyer chose you. It may not reside in your core products or services. It may be hidden somewhere else. But it's there. Look closer and you should be able to find its source, extract its value, and capture it in your pricing. And for God's sake, stop using the C-word. If you're pressed to refer to some commodity-like features of your offering, talk about general-purpose products or high-volume specialties instead. In the context of pricing, *commodity* is just another word for "lack of imagination."

Myth: You Should Never Take Leadership in Pricing

A lot has been said about the potential risks and challenges of deploying enterprise-wide pricing software platforms. Some experts recommend that companies wait for other players in their industry to deploy and integrate emerging pricing software technologies first and learn from their experience. Let the pioneers take the arrows, they say—be a follower, and you'll get the benefit of their experience indirectly and have a much easier time integrating the pricing technology. As you can imagine, I disagree with this position. In my experience, an organization that operates in an industry where price optimization software is not yet deployed has a unique opportunity to take a strong leadership position by moving first.

In my research, I have also found a strong positive relationship between the design and creation of pricing capabilities and overall firm performance, capabilities that typically include the deployment and assimilation of enterprise-level pricing software. Deploying a uniquely designed price optimization solution creates a strategic advantage that cannot be easily matched. Data shows that it also delivers a tremendous bang to the bottom line. When pricing software is deployed, when relevant pricing skills are built, and when the CEO championing the pricing process is resolute, the company can gain a unique and inimitable competitive advantage. Being the first company in an industry to deploy a pricing optimization solution is a great way to capture more value in the market and to educate the industry on the benefit of greater pricing realization, which will make it less likely that the industry will start a destructive price war.

Of course, this level of commitment isn't for everybody. Being first in an industry to deploy an advanced pricing process requires a long-term commitment from top leadership. Like any software implementation, you have to take this project seriously and make sure the up-front work (the blueprint design, pricing process mapping, and change management) is complete and thorough. You will need to put some of your company's best minds on the problem. But it's worth the trouble; you owe it to your employees, your shareholders, and most of all, your customers, to become the best-in-class player in your industry in value and pricing management. Academic and industry data both show that if you do this successfully, your bottom line will be improved, your employers and shareholders will be happier, and your customers' satisfaction levels will go up. How often does any company have an opportunity to do all of those things at once?

Myth: We Do Not Have a Problem of Pricing Irrationality

No one creates myths on purpose. Most business leaders and pricing practitioners believe their pricing decisions are grounded in experience, derived from data, and not subject to irrationality. In reality, pricing irrationality is one of pricing's biggest enemies. At least six kinds of irrationality can and do lead frequently to bad pricing decisions:

Uncertainty and ambiguity. Leaders, like most of us, hate uncertainty, dislike ambiguity, and cannot handle complexity. As a result, Simon (1961:93) posits that the behavior of leaders making decisions or making choices falls short of objective rationality in three ways: (1) incompleteness of knowledge, 2) difficulty in anticipating the consequences that will follow a choice; and (3) the challenge of making one choice among all possible alternative behaviors. These limitations constitute what scholars call *bounded rationality*, which means that otherwise rational leaders are significantly constrained by limitations of information and insight (Cyert and March 1992:214). The field of pricing is full of ambiguous and subjective data. Competitors' new prices are heard through the grapevine. Data from customer surveys may be read in different ways. That creates an environment of uncertainty and ambiguity that managers in firms must deal with on a daily basis. And the more uncertain the environment gets, the more likely that leaders will turn from objective parameters to intuitive and subjective ones (Daft and Weick 1984). If the model doesn't seem to be working, they will turn away from it. They will try to simplify complex strategic pricing issues and soothe their anxiety by inventing "a rationality, a recipe or an interpretative scheme" (Brownlie and Spender 1995) to make their decisions.

Information and systems breakdown. The way pricing information enters and is transmitted throughout the organization (Cyert and March 1992:79), how it is interpreted (Daft and Weick 1984), and how it is used (Ingenbleek 2007) can also lead to gaps in pricing rationality. Again, the more gaps managers have in their understanding of the outside world, the more they will try to fill those holes with intuition, invention, and irrational interpretations (Daft and Weick 1984). Bias in information-handling rules (Cyert and March 1992:123) will also creep in because of "perceptual differences among the subunits of the firm" (Cyert and March 1992:79). These information-handling rules include both routing rules (who will communicate to whom about what) and filtering rules (what will be communicated and under what form) (Cyert and March 1992:129). The rigidity of the rules and the manager's experience will also affect how the organization deploys valuable information (Ingenbleek 2007; Porac, Thomas, and

Baden-Fuller 1989). If as a leader you make it clear that you don't appreciate bad news or have a worldview that doesn't permit inconvenient truths,
your subordinates will eventually take the hint and not bring them to you
anymore.

Organizational routines, rules, and recipes. The brain tends to impose
order whether that order exists or not. We find faces in clouds and see the
future in tea leaves. The same phenomenon happens on a large scale in
organizations. To make sense of conflicting signals, teams impose routines,
standardize operating procedures, follow industry traditions and practices, develop information-handling rules, and make risk-avoiding agreements that reduce uncertainty in the choices they make and the goals they
set (Cyert and March 1992:38). Such routines can make it easier to cope
with uncertainty, but they can also put organizations on automatic pilot
(Langer 1989), preventing them from considering information that lies
outside the decision's traditional parameters. Value recipes (Matthyssens,
Vandenbempt, and Berghman 2006), for instance, may limit a firm's ability
to experiment with innovative pricing methods (Spender 1989; Cyert and
March 1992:124) and encourage managers to copy problem-solving recipes
within their industry. Ordinarily, routines, rules, and recipes create a script
of answers that help protect leaders from making irrational decisions. However, because of their static and inflexible nature, such heuristics can also
create a perception of irrationality for those on the receiving end of the
decision. Drawing standard and preexisting answers from this repertoire of
the organizational memory (Walsh and Ungson 1991) can lead to decisions
not aligned with the organization's goals and become a source of irrational
behavior in their own right.

Conflict and power struggles. Conflicts or disputes among departments
can result from a lack of alignment between subunit goals or a failed bar-
gaining process among potential coalition members to reach a joint negotiated goal (March, Simon, and Guetzkow 1958:60; Cyert and March 1992:50).
For example, marketing, finance, and sales departments often conflict on
whether profit should be maximized at the risk of impacting customers'
long-term relationships (Anderson, Wouters, and van Rossum 2010). Un-
resolved opposing views and priorities can lead some departments to resist
the adoption of progressive and aligned strategies (Lancioni, Schau, and

Smith 2005). These "power struggles and clan behaviors" (Dalton 1959:19) are based on a desire to control the strategic planning process (Lancioni, Schau, and Smith 2005). The finance departments traditionally see themselves as "the protectors of the firm's profitability." The accounting departments control the systems that provide accurate and relevant information (Lancioni, Schau, and Smith 2005). When multiple parties are involved in the decision-making process, frictional conflicts (Pondy 1969), disputes, disagreements, and passionate discussions occur (Dutta, Zbaracki, and Bergen 2003). In response to these frictions, the firm defines routines and mechanisms to avoid and resolve them, and requires a broader coordination mechanism across the groups involved in the decision-making process (Brandenburger and Stuart 1996). Over time, these learned and adaptive resolution routines become a critical resource to the firm (Dutta, Zbaracki, and Bergen 2003). However, don't expect 100 percent support. In fact, 100 percent enthusiasm would be a bad sign, as institutionalized conflicts are an important aspect of functional organizations (Lewicki, Weiss, and Lewin 1992). On the contrary, they are almost essential to their existence. Most long-lasting organizations have some kind of institutionalized conflict built into their structure (Pondy 1992).

Competitive irrationality. In many industries, competition can be fierce. Managers can become overwhelmed by the amount of competitive information and the number of decisions they must make (Dutta, Zbaracki, and Bergen 2003). The level of competitive intensity in a market can require fast reaction times and a strong capability to respond adequately and in a timely manner. Increases in competitive activities may generate more irrationality, uncertainty, and "unanalyzability" of market information (Daft and Weick 1984), leading to an increase in organizational stress. Besides the potentially disruptive and stressful relationship between competitive intensity and decision-making behaviors, continued intense competitive rivalry may create long-term behaviors that encourage competitive irrationality. For example, companies sometimes focus on damaging competitors' profits (Graf et al. 2012) while ignoring the costs to themselves—such as the classic case of Kmart choosing to start a price war against Walmart, although Walmart was the more efficient competitor. An expensive acquisition to capture a new market can earn you a similar Pyrrhic victory. You may win in the short run, but the high fives and chest bumps of your "win" may come back to haunt you later on.

Intuition and gut feeling in decision making. While some intuitive influences are generally expected in business and decision-making behaviors, many decisions in firms are made because "it felt good," "it felt all right," or they had gone around the room and gathered "collective intuition" from participants. This isn't entirely wrong. Intuition may be an appropriate element of decision making in certain situations and business scenarios. It can be especially useful in situations of uncertainty or turbulence (Khatri and Ng 2000), novelty situations, or situations related to human resources. Scholars liken the intuitive skills of managers to the intuitive skills of chess masters or physicians (Simon 1987). While a few leaders are able to combine both approaches to reach a greater level of decision effectiveness (Dane and Pratt 2007; Simon 1987), many are not able to weigh evidence against experience very well and instead ignore the evidence and use pure gut feel or impulse to make significant firm decisions. In the words of one executive I interviewed, "making a decision is playing Russian roulette" (Liozu et al. 2011).

Conclusions

As the pricing function has evolved, so have pricing myths. Yet many of these myths still paralyze the progression of pricing knowledge in the business world and the development of pricing capabilities. The pricing function needs to fight and address each of these myths one by one so that managers see the true face and potential of pricing. How do we do this? By publishing books and promoting them in the marketing mainstream world; by focusing more of our efforts not on the current generation of leaders, who may be difficult to convince, but on the next generation— younger dogs more open to new tricks—who are open-minded enough to hear you when you say that pricing is the only revenue-generating element of marketing's famous four *P*s (product, price, promotion, and place); and by creating a community of "pricing evangelists" who have the courage and the resilience to promote the art and science of pricing.

10 Pricing Skills to Face Complexity and Dynamic Environments

The task of managing large and sometimes complex pricing transformations as described in the previous chapters requires skills, experience, and a high level of leadership maturity. Pricing professionals have to manage multiple road maps, internal and external environments, difficult cultural components, and a lot of moving parts. They aren't the sorts of skills you can just wing; you have to learn them. Today's technical and analytical skills are certainly well covered by many of the training courses available from the Professional Pricing Society and other elective courses as part of MBA programs. However, training programs for softer skills and pricing future skills are scarce and mostly acquired by working on specific pricing projects.

To add to the complexity, the skills that pricing experts need to know keep changing. Over the past twenty years, pricing has evolved from a clerical and tactical function to a complex system that incorporates advanced technology and behavioral developments. As the pricing task changed, the skills that pricing practitioners needed changed too. Pricing is no longer about filing pricing conditions or entering data in legacy systems. Technology has taken over more and more of the predictive analytics and optimization work over the past 10 years, and most analysts expect that trend to continue. Technology has transformed the game—and over the next 20 years, it will play an increasingly important role in pricing decision making.

However, this doesn't mean pricing will be easy. No one can forecast exactly how the technology will develop, but it is safe to say that as the systems advance, they will likely create new and increasingly complex sets of risks. Dynamic markets, complex communication and interpretation systems, inefficient organizational structures, fragmented systems, Big Data, market microsegmentation, pricing variations between channels, organizational inertia, lack of a common vocabulary, and internal power struggles are all but certain to create unexpected crises that will test pricing leaders' abilities in a variety of ways. In other words, the good news is that you no longer have to worry about your old Chevy's brakes and whether the starter is going to die. The bad news is that now you have to learn to fly a 747.

In this chapter, we will look at what this historic shift is likely to mean, and I will venture some guesses about how pricing practitioners might best prepare the next generation to cope with these exciting but complex opportunities.

The Emergence of Pricing Technology

In a few years, most pricing analytics will almost certainly be managed with advanced algorithms run by some form of superior computing intelligence. As in so many fields, this will have a counterintuitive result; instead of turning pricing practitioners into programmers, the advances in technology will likely lead pricing practitioners to spend less time on pricing's technical side. With more analytics running on autopilot and an ever-increasing range of decisions made by supercomputers mining Big Data, the pricing executive's work will focus instead on the social, behavioral, and emotional dimensions of the deployment of pricing programs in their organizations. As in so many professions, the pricing professionals' focus will shift from quantitative and analytical "left-brain" skills to intuitive and emotional "right-brain" skills (Figure 10.1).

The Balance Between Hard and Soft Skills

Many of today's basic pricing skills involve learning how to run manual analytics, Excel models, and tools. A lot of effort is also expended trying to compensate for poor system interfaces and fragmented data. Tomorrow, all these Scotch-tape-and-chicken-wire processes will be gone. Analyt-

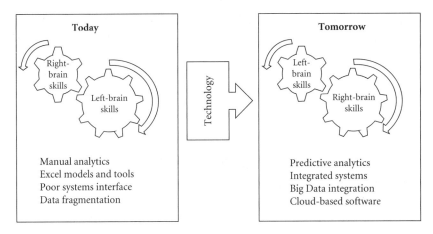

Figure 10.1 How technology is changing pricing

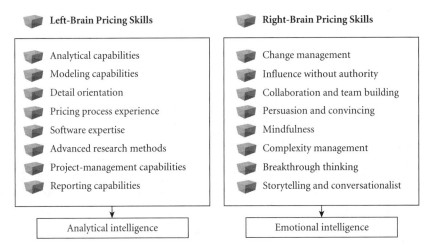

Figure 10.2 A balance of skills

ics will be predictive and drawn from integrated systems, integrated data, and cloud-based software. Left-brain capabilities (see Figure 10.2) such as analytical and modeling skills, detail orientation, process understanding, software expertise, advanced research method skills, project management capabilities, and reporting capabilities will matter, somewhat less than they do now. Right-brain emotional intelligence skills such as change management, complexity management, and persuasive, collaborative, and team-building skills will matter more. The pricing agents of today and tomorrow will need to be creative storytellers—good conversationalists who can also make the occasional analytical breakthrough.

One counterintuitive result of the rise of analytics is that pricing agents' ability to make a case for particular pricing drivers will depend more on personal persuasion than ever. With objective values all worked out in nanoseconds, the importance of subjective values will rise. In an odd way, we will have gone full circle back to the days of the bazaar, when buyers and sellers haggled over prices over tea.

For pricing managers, this shift requires some important changes in their curriculum. The right-brain pricing skills shown in Figure 10.2 are not as easily learned and absorbed as some of the more analytical and quantitative skills. It is not reasonable to expect that you can attend an afternoon seminar and become a breakthrough thinker by the end of the day. Most right-brain skills are learned through experience and through interaction with other functions in the firm. For example, working closely with the sales force and learning some of their selling skills can certainly help teach pricing practitioners to be more persuasive. One consequence of this shift is that pricing practitioners are spending more time on the road, visiting customers to learn the sales vocabulary and see firsthand how pricing applications are being used in the field.

Professional organizations such as the American Marketing Association and the Professional Pricing Society are already helping with this transition by offering a new set of webinars, courses, and certifications in "softer" disciplines. They offer, for example, workshops on change management and strategic thinking. Human resources and organizational development departments will also play a crucial role in equipping the current generation of pricing professionals with the right sets of change and emotional skills. In fact, it's already happening; over the past few years, many Fortune 500 companies have created business transformation positions to support organizational transformations. Johnson Controls, for example, has entire business transformation teams supporting various departments. Syngenta calls some of its pricing professionals "Global Pricing Transformation Consultants." Coca-Cola Enterprises use the title of "Business Process Professional." Castrol/BP adopted the title of "Marketing Transformation Manager," and Apple prefers "Business Process Reengineering Analyst."

Pricing educators face an even greater challenge. Right now, schools that offer a pricing elective tend to gear it heavily toward analytics, tactics, economic models, and occasionally pricing strategies. Missing from the curriculum are important aspects of pricing in the areas of organizational theory, behavioral science, and the psychology of pricing. However, this disconnection won't last forever. The growing importance of skills that improve emotional intelligence will eventually force a change not only in the pricing curriculum of business schools but also in corporate training programs generally. Sooner or later, we are sure to see more right-brain skills taught in MBA courses, in the Professional Pricing Society certification process, and in consultants' training modules. Advanced pricing simply can't function without them.

However, pricing professionals won't get out of analytics completely—they will need to know enough statistics to keep up with the Big Data revolution. At the same time, the most successful pricing professionals will need to be able to move outside their traditional boundaries and learn about sales and marketing concepts: segmentation, sales force effectiveness, consumer behaviors, and more. This implies embracing more complexity and being able to integrate it as part of the job description, which as we shall see is much easier said than done.

Managing the Complexity of Value and Pricing Management

As I have mentioned before, one of the critical elements of the organizational journey toward pricing excellence is the organization's capacity for change. Moving from a formula-based pricing orientation to a customer-value orientation requires deep changes and an overall organizational mobilization directed toward the desired goal (Liozu et al. 2011). This transformation also requires the management of numerous moving parts at the same time, even as they work with stakeholders who may have conflicting objectives. A pricing transformation is a complex exercise that cannot be considered without understanding the foundation of complexity management.

Managing Complexity

Pricing managers will need to learn how to manage the sort of complex system that Richard Boyatzis describes as a "multi-level combination of systems that may behave in a way independent of any one of the component systems" (2006:608). In fact, pricing management is even more tangled than most complex systems, as it crosses various levels, multiple dimensions, and multiple cultures and requires the convergence of multiple languages within the organization (Figure 10.3). In order for their organization to reach what I call the C^4 *zone*, becoming an organization where convergence, collaboration, conversation, and consensus thrive, pricing professionals will have to acquire a number of important intellectual and social skills that do not come prepackaged in any off-the-shelf training program. Not even a prior career in traditional pricing can prepare them to manage the inherent complexity the new pricing management will entail. In fact, a prior life in marketing, sales, or finance may prove to be a better preparation for tomorrow's pricing assignments than today's price-management training.

Any pricing policy is already the result of complex interactions between internal subsystems (functions and departments) that are themselves

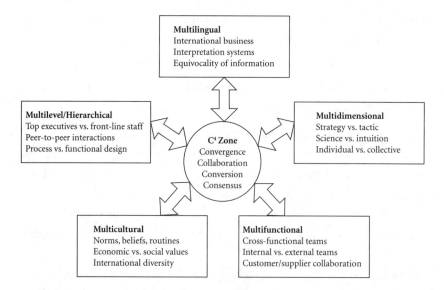

Figure 10.3 The complexity of pricing

exposed to internal and external opposition, but those interactions will become more and more intense in the coming years. As all these agents and actors act independently, tensions, conflicts, misunderstandings, negotiations, and arguments will be par for the course. The process leaves plenty of room for failure, poor decision making, irrational behaviors, and breakdowns. No wonder managers who attempt to deploy advanced pricing programs often "throw in the towel" early.

Fortunately, there will be some good examples to follow. Firms that are competent in pricing have developed more sophisticated ways of price setting (Dutta et al. 2002). First, they adopt a pricing orientation and engage in advanced pricing practices. These practices refer to the set of well-orchestrated activities and behaviors executed by an organization's managers that lead to the pricing decision. One such step is to create a special zone where relevant pricing decision makers and agents can converge in order to start collaborating in a value and pricing conversation. Eventually, these decision makers must reach some kind of consensus that leads them to discuss value, increase organizational buy-in, and generate positive energy about the decision.

This requires what Boyatzis describes as *resonant leadership* (Boyatzis and McKee 2005)—the direction of leaders who can work across multiple levels, multiple functions, and multiple dimensions to create the necessary degree of productive interactions among teams. They need to be able to capture the influence and power of the various groups involved in pricing (Lancioni, Schau, and Smith 2005) and create coalitions. Only by building consensus and enthusiasm can they build greater collective confidence in implementing the pricing vision (Kanter 2006; Liozu et al. 2011; Bohn 2002).

The journey to pricing excellence is a complex transformation that requires experimentation, teamwork, difficult decisions, and significant investments. Along the way, pricing professionals must become agents of change, driving transformation by managing successes as well as failures. They must be able to sort through complexity and translate difficult tasks into simpler but still accurate propositions. Today's growth in computing power makes the "hard" analytical issues simpler to resolve but also makes "soft" issues increasingly complex.

Dynamic Systems Dimension

Markets are not static. They tend to be dynamic and require organizational adaptations and a certain capacity to absorb, react, and change (Meyer and Stensaker 2006). The porous boundaries of industries and market sectors are affected by mergers and acquisitions, new market entrants, aggressive penetration strategies, and government regulations—all elements that add phenomenal levels of turbulence into business ecosystems.

The inherent complexity created by such dynamic, complex systems forces organizations to keep bending and reshaping their organizational architecture. Pricing and value functions cannot escape change as industry structures morph, commoditization accelerates, and innovation disrupts a business sector (Matthyssens, Vandenbempt, and Berghman 2006). Many industries (e.g., airlines, e-commerce, and hospitality) have reacted to such turbulence by investing heavily in dynamic pricing approaches and advanced revenue- and yield-management programs. In such industries, the question becomes not so much how to control the system as how to anticipate system dynamics and adapt proactively to the market's swings.

Complex Communication and Interpretation Systems

Individuals in organizations are forced to make decisions based on insufficient information all the time (Tushman and Scanlan 1981). But while the gaps in cost and competitive information can usually be extrapolated mathematically, information relating to customer value is often subjective (Hinterhuber 2008b) and ambiguous. Gathering value-related information requires the use of market research techniques such as focus groups, surveys, field value-in-use assessments, conjoint analysis (Anderson, Jain, and Chintagunta 1993), and environmental scanning. Empirical studies have suggested that difficulties in gathering customer information are related to finding the right respondents and handling "soft" attributes effectively (Anderson, Jain, and Chintagunta 1993; Hinterhuber 2008a).

Of course, the availability of customer value information alone does not guarantee success. How information is transmitted throughout the organization (Cyert and March 1992:79), how it is interpreted (Daft and Weick 1984), and how it is used (Ingenbleek 2007) are also important considerations. As Daft and Weick (1984) observed, interpretation is what gives meaning to data.

Several factors may affect the complexity of interpretation. First, the meaning of the data may not be all that clear and subject to conflicting readings (Daft and Macintosh 1981). Second, the data-gathering process itself may encourage a particular slant on the data (Daft and Weick 1984). As critical pricing information about costs, competition, and customer value circulate through the organization and reach decision makers, interpretation filters and information-handling rules always affect the way data is finally assembled to support key pricing decisions.

Third, the capacity to measure information raises the level of uncertainty in the decision-making process (Spender 1989:188). Of the five elements included in the definition of customer value, only three are directly measurable: benefits expressed in monetary terms, costs expressed in monetary terms, and price. The other two, perceived benefits and costs, can't be easily expressed as single sets of numbers, which makes customer value assessment an inherently uncertain exercise (Anderson, Kumar, and Narus 2007:23). Fourth, the complexity of the larger market can also raise the level of uncertainty and ambiguity in the decision-making process (Duncan 1972). As the environment grows more complex, managers will shift their assessment from objective parameters to intuitive and subjective judgments, inventions, and manipulations (Daft and Weick 1984).

Gaps in communication may also affect interactions. Suppliers must be able to recode their language in terms that are useful to the customer. Their sales reps must adopt a language based not on product features and attributes but on customer benefits and emotional attractors. A strong alignment of language with all the relevant stakeholders is necessary to keep multiple and conflicting interpretations to a minimum.

Organizations often add complexity to their processes and business practices without taking a step back from time to time to assess whether this complexity is adding value. This may be especially true in pricing management, which touches multiple silos and levels of an organization. Conducting a pricing transformation in a context of intense complexity always raises the risk of failure and forces many internal problems to rise to the surface. For the most part, pricing complexity arises in eight different ways:

1. *Inefficient organizational structure.* In many firms, pricing is a fragmented process divided among various departments. The result is a constant state of interaction and discussion between the finance, marketing, and sales departments, none of whom have clear responsibilities and accountability (Lancioni, Schau, and Smith 2005; Liozu et al. 2011). Their inherent struggles impede the pricing process and lead either to conflict or to a false consensus based on internal conflict avoidance (Pfeffer 1994; Cyert and March 1992) rather than market needs.

2. *Fragmented systems.* The emergence of integrated price-optimization systems has reduced connectivity problems between enterprise resource software and price-management software. However, many firms still suffer from complex software infrastructures that do not communicate well with each other. Suboptimal software reduces the ability of managers to make appropriate pricing decisions based on integrated and logical consolidated data. To cope, pricing teams often develop complex manual workarounds to support pricing decision making—a situation that is growing increasingly acute because of the demand for information driven by Big Data analytics.

3. *Big Data.* Organizations now manage and maintain millions of price data and pricing-condition statistics. Some are created automatically through the generation of pricing conditions during order entry. Others must be inputted manually during the construction of competitive pricing databases. This creates a complex analytical challenge for pricing professionals as they develop exploratory and explanatory models to generate optimal pricing levels.

4. *Microsegmentation.* The adoption of value-based pricing requires a very strong up-front focus on the segmentation process in order to gauge the customer's willingness to pay (Hinterhuber 2004; Anderson and Narus 1998). However, you can end up with too much of a

good thing; a serious segmentation analysis may drill down to such a granular level that you end up with thousands of price segments and conditions, adding an unmanageable level of complexity.

5. *Pricing "Turkish bazaar" style.* The management of pricing through multiple channels requires a solid organizational structure and advanced price-management systems. Previous research revealed that the complexity of managing price conditions through multiple channels acts as a stimulus to change the overall pricing orientation (Liozu, Hinterhuber, Perelli, et al. 2012). When prices are not structured and consistent across channel segments, customers may take advantage of the situation or feel frustrated and dissatisfied, and become so focused on the price that they overlook the value of the product.

6. *Organizational inertia.* Organizational inertia in the face of dynamic environmental changes leads to a serious disconnect between the action needed to respond to a change and the actual response. Inertia and a general resistance to change leads to quick fixes, manual workarounds, and organizational kludges (Duymedjian and Rüling 2010), all of which add greater complexity to pricing tasks and routines.

7. *Meaning of value and pricing.* Few firms invest in training programs that teach everyone the fundamentals of pricing and value management. Without a common vocabulary on such core concepts as cost, value, and price, leaders and decision makers tend to experience a lot of frustration when they try to develop a common pricing strategy.

8. *A question of control.* The debate over the delegation of pricing authority rages on. Scholars are divided on the subject of what positively influences pricing realization (Frenzen et al. 2010). However, they agree that pricing authority cannot be fully delegated to sales personnel without some type of controlling structure in place and without strong investments in training and capability-building activities (Liozu et al. 2011). Giving sales personnel full pricing authority can lead to the creation of numerous pricing and service

conditions. The resulting incremental complexity may not be easily managed in existing information systems and can quickly deteriorate margins while draining administrative resources.

I think I have made a strong point for the need for more skills to manage the increasing level of complexity. But what does it mean to manage pricing complexity? What do you manage it for? In fact, how can pricing professionals leverage the management of complexity in data, science, behaviors, and systems management so that they make a difference in the organization?

Leveraging Organizational Complexity for Differentiation

Organizations will need to improve their capacity to manage complexity as pricing teams integrate ever more technologies, data, and intelligent systems in their decisions (Dutta et al. 2002). Logically, this means that the success of pricing managers will depend on the degree to which they meld the strength of human behavior with the power of intelligent systems. However, as always, reaching that goal is not easy. Faced with increased complexity in pricing and value management, managers often abdicate their pricing power and try to stitch decisions together using the resources and skills at hand (Steffens, Senyard, and Baker 2009). The more difficult, but ultimately more advantageous, path is to take a proactive and dynamic approach to understand the roots of this complexity and leverage prices in a way that creates differentiation. If you choose that route, you will need to do the following:

Identify the "hot spots" of pricing complexity. As part of a regular pricing capability assessment, you will need to conduct a pricing complexity audit to capture the "hot spots" associated with wasted resources, manual workarounds, inefficient processes, inconsistent data analysis, and irrational pricing patterns. Such an audit can be conducted only as part of an annual audit of the larger business. By capturing the hot spots of pricing complexity, leaders can engage in deeper discussions about how to transform that complexity into a productive force for the organization.

Remove illogical legacy pricing principles and unnecessary pricing complexity. Addressing complex issues must be a priority for top leaders, especially when these come from legacy management practices that represent organizational sacred cows. Building pricing capabilities atop broken legacy processes or principles can be counterproductive. A pricing capability audit combined with supportive internal and customer surveys of how a firm's pricing strategies are perceived will quickly uncover unnecessary and unproductive pricing complexity hidden in subprocesses, rules, and guidelines.

Embrace designed complexity to create differentiation. The real challenge of complexity management in pricing is to develop productive complexity. Productive pricing complexity may include creative pricing strategies that help capture more value, better systems that intelligently integrate and optimize all available data, or an organizational structure that appears to be counterintuitive but supports commercial personnel more effectively. Pricing and value professionals can also create differentiation by designing unique pricing tools, interactive models, value models, pricing conditions, and messages that create excitement with their commercial personnel and their customers and generate greater pricing power. The trick here is to create complexity that generates value rather than analytics for analytics' sake.

Develop sustainable pricing capabilities. Complexity management must be part of the pricing and value management training curriculum. Ambidextrous capabilities—the ability to tolerate ambiguity and actively manage complexity at the same time—can enable employees to create and use networks within organizations to build relationships and help overcome poor processes, bridge organizational silos, or manage whatever value-creating pockets of complexity their companies decide to maintain (Birkinshaw and Heywood 2010). As complexity continues to increase decade after decade, driven by the increasing globalization of business and the adoption of superior technologies, investments in complexity-related training must be maintained to keep the pricing system sustainable.

Encourage systemic thinking and superior design. Managing complexity
is a real design challenge for leaders of organizations as marketers
and business strategists develop programs that involve co-creation
with different business units, partnerships, and clients. As marketing strategies include ever more innovative modes of value creation
and collaboration, pricing and value-capture strategies should
reflect the company's latest thinking. Pricing systems may include
advanced bundling options; creative pricing menus that combine
products, parts, and services; dynamic pricing algorithms; and new
pricing and value models based on customer research. There is no
reason why creativity and design in pricing should not be as powerful as the creativity and design employed in product and packaging
programs. The only barrier is the "iron cage" of traditional cost-
based analysis that keeps creativity out of pricing.

As complexity in pricing increases inside and outside the organization,
human resources and organizational development departments in firms
may have to start developing a new training agenda. For example, as General Electric is moving from being a pure manufacturer of things to being a
provider of services and software, its training agenda will evolve too. Pricing analytics based on crunching the data gathered by information gathered by millions of sensors is not the same as pricing a jet engine! But as
business models evolve, so will pricing models—and that requires training.

The New Training Agenda

Looking ahead, pricing seems likely to follow the same evolution as so
many technical disciplines where the technical aspects that once occupied
most practitioners' days become a relatively small part of the job for all but
a few advanced specialists. For most pricing executives, quantitative analytics will eventually become less important than qualitative analytics, and
programs in pricing and value will need to be more progressive, creative,
and interactive.

To meet that challenge, companies and schools should begin to rethink
their pricing curriculums now and supplement their traditional analytic

training with the social and emotional skills that can help them develop the kind of leaders that companies that follow advanced pricing approaches will need. I recommend the following five areas as critical components of any future pricing training curriculum:

1. *Change management.* Pricing professionals should be familiar with the most commonly used change-management methodologies and theories. They should pursue change-management certification as soon as possible in order to begin to include these methods right away in their pricing initiatives.

2. *Complexity management.* Pricing professionals should learn the basic concepts of complexity theory in order to better manage complex problems, complex designs, and complex transformation programs.

3. *Emotional intelligence.* There are many books and courses on the value of emotional intelligence in organizations. This is not a new concept but it is evolving rapidly, and the best behavioral scientists in the world are conducting additional research on it.

4. *Leadership essentials.* Pricing professionals should be required to take basic leadership training from the get-go, either while still in school or when they start their mission. Leading a pricing and value management program requires some crucial leadership skills: leading teams, leading without formal authority, listening, and communicating with power.

5. *Design and system thinking.* Last but not least, a transformation program is first and foremost a road map toward pricing excellence. As such, it requires skills in the area of sociotechnical systems and sociotechnical design. You cannot design a road map over several years that involves dozens of moving parts without advanced skills and knowledge.

Conclusion

The skills needed to manage a pricing transformation are changing in nature and intellectual intensity. Soon, understanding how to program and model in Excel won't be nearly enough. As technologies evolve and take over some of the more basic components of today's job descriptions, pricing professionals will need to learn the skills to handle these new complex challenges. If you're a pricing professional who wants to stay relevant, you should ask yourself two simple questions: Am I doing enough today to learn and acquire these skills? Am I planning ahead for myself or am I depending on my organization to give me the skills I will need in the future?

11 Closing Thoughts

I wrote this book for executives to help them design and implement better pricing strategies. Many of the points in the 5C model are not new. Schneider Electric, DuPont, Eastman Chemicals, Grainger, GE, Philips, and other leading companies have all used pricing capabilities, center-led pricing, and executive sponsorship to move their pricing practices forward. What is different in the 5C model is the recognition that change management and collective confidence are critical elements to accelerate and assimilate new pricing technologies. But cookie-cutter is not one of the Cs: only a unique combination of the five factors, tailored for your organization's needs, will create the right conditions for a true pricing transformation. Orchestrated by a strong and passionate champion at the top, the design and deployment of a unique organizational architecture for pricing can boost the organization's collective intellectual power and transformational drive. Add to these elements a sound business strategy and a progressive human capital management program, and your organization will produce miracles in bottom-line performance.

I began this book talking about how my experience as a young executive at Owens Corning in Europe transformed my outlook about pricing. Now I want to close it with my most recent executive position—my tenure as CEO of ARDEX Americas from 2008 to 2012—and what it taught me about the value of the 5C model.

The Case of ARDEX Americas

As the new CEO of ARDEX Americas, I was once again brought in at a difficult moment: just six months before the recession began in 2008. Already, we were facing a total market collapse, including a drop in volume of up to 40 percent in some categories; a shift in customer value perceptions from the high end to the middle end of the market; and incredible competitive pressure across all customer segments. I knew that better pricing would be key to our survival but that we couldn't take the time I would have liked to make the transition easier. Everything had to be done yesterday.

Faced with a formidable economic collapse, our team decided to take a proactive approach and to embark on a pricing transformation. Our journey on the Pricing Capability Grid (see Figure 11.1) started with improving our pricing process and putting in place a progressive pricing organization—in other words, we moved right before we moved up. Our road map consisted of four major steps:

1. *Increase the focus on pricing.* Inject knowledge on value management, design necessary reports, and make the case for more attention to pricing by identifying the challenges that needed to be fixed over time (18 months).

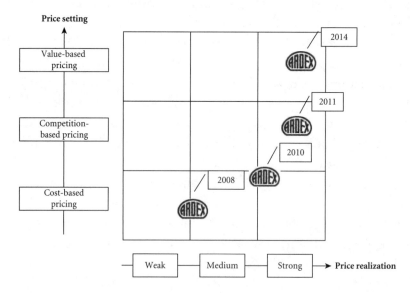

Figure 11.1 The ARDEX Americas journey

2. *Formalize the pricing process.* Create the pricing team with dedicated experts who manage pricing and revenue optimization, invest a great deal in training, design and launch the pricing council, deploy price realization plans, and start the training on value-based pricing (18 months).

3. *Invest in the fundamentals of value-based pricing.* Formalize the pricing process for all new products, conduct training in value-based pricing for the entire organization, track customers' value perceptions as well as competitive position using value maps, and revisit customer segmentation with good/better/best strategic options (12 months).

4. *Focus on execution and productivity improvements.* Deploy relevant software to accelerate our value-based pricing process, and develop a unique training program for the sales force to develop their value-capture confidence (ongoing).

As the project's champion, I drove the transformation process with passion and energy. I spent quite a bit of time in the design and initiative stages of the road map definition and I allocated the best talent to the pricing function, making sure resources were available even though we were in the middle of a severe economic recession. Pricing was everywhere; we discussed it in management team meetings, in sales force interactions, in budget discussions. I made sure that the topic was known widely and was part of all strategic discussions. No one could doubt that the executive team had made pricing excellence a strategic priority for our organization. We also made sure our investments in pricing training, tools, and processes were significant and continuous. I wanted to build long-term capabilities and develop all skills from the inside with adequate support from consultants when needed; by the time I left, we had over 25 Certified Pricing Professionals in ARDEX Americas. Every sales professional received significant pricing and value training, including training on differentiation versus competitors. Training came from sales leadership, which in turn increased credibility and ownership.

From the get-go, we decided to adopt a center-led management design, setting up a group of pricing specialists to support the transformation who shared overall pricing execution authority with the sales leadership. We allocated the best talent in the pricing team to run the pricing council. This worked well: our design for the pricing council made a significant impact on our ability to create a winning coalition for change across the organization. Pricing and sales were a winning team.

My pricing team implemented the change incrementally, and I brought everyone along through coaching, training, and the development and communication of a shared vision. This took five years, ultimately, but speed did not matter for me as a CEO. What mattered was the level of organizational change and the assimilation of critical value and pricing concepts across the firm. We took our time and worked in steps when the organization was ready. The combination of change-management science and the change leadership by all the executive team allowed us to significantly and sustainably transform the organization's DNA.

When we reached Stage 4 of our transformation, we recognized the need to shore up the company's pricing confidence. This is probably where we experienced the greatest challenge to our transformation. The sales force was in the field and often disconnected from headquarters. The competitive pressures were tremendous and slowed down our ability to face customers with greater confidence. Looking at the value-capture confidence revolution presented earlier in the book, I realize that we could have paid more attention to some of these programs. At the time, the best we could do, however, was to design a specific training program that combined on-site, in-the-field, and online training.

Still, the 5C model of transformation worked for us. The combination of these five organizational elements and a strong strategic orientation allowed us to capture more value in and from the market. In fact, we managed to do so while navigating through the worst economic recession in years. Our focus on strategic pricing was intentional, coordinated, and relentless. As a team, we learned some useful lessons along the way, including the importance of staying the course, finding a training "sherpa" to lead the process, and keeping management focused on the project. Finally, we learned that although our process started in finance, it inevitably ended up in marketing. Pricing excellence leads to increased understanding of customer value.

In late 2012, ARDEX Americas entered the Pricing Power Zone. Our journey on the Pricing Capability Grid had taken four years and was still not complete—but it had gone far enough that when I left ARDEX at the end of that year to found my own pricing consulting firm, I was confident that we had achieved a permanent change in the company's pricing orientation. Our DNA was transformed from a cost-based organization to a value-based company with a deeper understanding of customer value, cost excellence, and competition. Customer value was at the heart of our reenergized value-based innovation and value-based marketing strategies.

Pricing clearly improved our bottom line. When combined with other strategic business initiatives, it created a source of additional revenue and profit that helped justify greater investments by our shareholders. The stories of ARDEX Americas and dozens of companies who have successfully done pricing transformations teach us many important lessons. As a matter of fact, I propose these in the next section in the form of a manifesto for change-driven pricing.

A Manifesto for Change-Driven Pricing

1. Learning Is at the Heart of Change

As project leader, you have to know nearly everything there is to know about pricing and value management. Focus on learning the various languages that are spoken by your internal and external stakeholders (clients, distributors, sales reps, operations, and more). Because pricing is a multidisciplinary function, you also have to develop your overall business acumen by learning more about fields like finance, customer fulfillment, supply chains, and R&D. Finally, you will need to know how to teach and sell your thoughts, ideas, and projects to others inside and outside the organization. If you lead the overall pricing transformation, knowing more about the art of persuasion and how to influence others when you lack the authority to compel them will become essential.

2. You Must Design Your Own Road Map

Consultants will be a great resource to help you design your overall road map and recommend the tools and capabilities you will need to reach your goals, but make sure you get one designed specifically for your company. Each road map must be unique and based on your pricing maturity level, industry dynamics, and internal culture. Avoid the "copy and paste" approach. Benchmarking how other organizations have done their pricing transformation can teach you a lot, but it won't give you a blueprint. Sometimes, this kind of imitation can even create an irrational sense of safety: "If DuPont did it this way, it will work for us too." My experience in the field and my discussions with numerous practitioners suggest that an incremental road map customized to your own business's challenges is a must-have for success. Your road map must also be a story of transformation that includes a vision of success and a clear before/after message. The story matters! You may have an easier time if you create a bit of drama in the beginning to reinforce the need for change.

3. Change Incrementally, Measure and Share Credit

I recently met with leaders of a privately held midsized organization in western Pennsylvania who wanted to discuss their pricing problems. The executives had formed a pricing committee but could not get it to approve any pricing projects. The internal resistance was so fierce that they could never get the buy-in they needed to move forward. I recommended they take a different approach and start small. If your culture is resistant to change, don't try to sell a complex and challenging pricing transformation. Break the project into bits and pieces and begin with incremental changes so you can measure their impact and promote their success. Once that is accomplished, repeat the exercise until you gain credibility and attention from top leaders. Success speaks for itself; eventually, someone at the top will notice. Finally, share the credit. When you give credit for success to colleagues in sales, marketing, or finance, you will help create a buzz for your approach and build confidence to take the next step.

4. Don't Rush

Seventy percent of change projects fail because users cannot absorb too much change at once (Liozu 2014). Pricing is already a difficult topic, and it is unrealistic to think that a commercial team, for example, can adopt a customer relationship management (CRM) platform, a price optimization solution, and a value-based pricing program in a twelve-month time frame. As a practitioner, you have to be able to gauge the rate of assimilation of your price setters and users to the new concepts, tools, and assets you give them. You will have to identify and use reliable metrics to track these as part of your change-management process. Some of the metrics may be quantitative (how many times does each sales rep enter the pricing analytical dashboard?), while others may be qualitative (value selling proficiency: green, yellow, and red). Don't move ahead until everyone in the company has caught up with you.

5. Pricing Is a Journey, Not a Destination

Pricing, like change generally, requires constant attention and investment. Change requires continual reinforcement through coaching, communication, and training. Customer perceptions evolve with time, and the competitive context changes frequently. Crises come and go. Organizations change as well; people leave and new people come in, and new units are required. Just when you think you are done, it starts all over again!

Why Does This Book Matter?

In the 1970s and 1980s, sociotechnical approaches gained in popularity and visibility around the world (Mumford 2006). Projects spread from manufacturing to service industries and seemed to herald a new social and human approach to management. However, by the early 1990s, these concepts had lost their appeal as a result of the emergence of stronger capitalistic forces that pushed sociotechnical theory toward a purely academic research agenda sprinkled with a few case studies. Today, as ethical and social considerations have gained a new focus, sociotechnical theory is undergoing a revival. My work clearly shows that sociotechnical concepts offer practical activities and resources that leaders can use to change the world and humanize the working environment.

   In this book, I have borrowed some of the most relevant concepts related to sociotechnical systems, sociotechnical change, and sociotechnical design and applied them to the field of pricing. My exploration reveals that the values and concepts of sociotechnical systems can have a powerful impact on firm performance. Many firms fail in their pricing transformation journey because they focus solely on the technical dimension of pricing, rather than the social and organizational dimensions, which are equally important. Most practitioners complain about the complexity of the pricing function (Dolan and Simon 1996; Lancioni 2005) but neglect to consider the kinds of complexity it creates. Often, they consider its technical complexity, but the complexity tends to stem from breakdowns in change management (Lyytinen and Newman 2008), difficult interactions between departments and teams (Lancioni, Schau, and Smith 2005), lack of support from top management (Hinterhuber 2008a), and a lack of confidence in the company's ability to capture value through pricing (Anderson, Kumar, and Narus 2007). Because pricing transformation is just as much a social and human challenge as a technical one, it follows that a sociotechnical framework can be a helpful way to consider the obstacles to a transformation.

This book also advances the theory of pricing capability as it relates to increased relative firm performance. Establishing a strong empirical and statistical link between pricing capabilities and firm performance provides strong support for investments in pricing. It also provides ammunition for pricing practitioners to justify these investments to top management and to help them compete against other functions who tend to win more investment dollars from the C-suite (R&D and manufacturing, for example). Another contribution is the demonstration that firms wishing to build organizational and strategic capabilities should focus attention and resources on both tangible and intangible capabilities. Building on the previous work from Dutta and colleagues (2002), we conclude that companies should pay equal attention to the organization design of superior capabilities that may lead to superior organizational intelligence and greater organizational capital in pricing, including systems, humans, and networks.

Another contribution of this work is the uncovering of the critical role that organizational confidence (Bohn 2001) in pricing plays as a key driver of a pricing transformation in firms and as a positive contributor to relative firm performance. While the concept of individual confidence and self-esteem is generally well understood by organizational development professionals, how to develop the collective self-esteem of teams is less frequently discussed. In fact, many of the books available to practitioners focus on helping build self-confidence and strengthen motivation, especially in the sales force. Elevating the level of analysis to the organization in the areas of change, confidence, and capabilities is a novel approach. In particular, prioritizing organizational confidence in pricing can change the way human capital is developed in firms. Our work shows that collective confidence does not stop with the sales force but needs to be extended to all functions implicated in the overall transformational project.

So why should you care? You should care because the pricing function is changing in a fast and furious manner. Business is getting more dynamic, competitive, and complex. The relationship between humans and machines is getting once again disrupted as technologies storm the field of pricing. Take it as a wake-up call! And pricing professionals are not alone. Our transformation model can be also applied to the field of Big Data, marketing automation, and supply chain management, for example.

As a pricing evangelist, I have tried to bring these theoretical and practical insights into the pricing profession. However, my model is only the beginning.

Where Do We Go from Here?

Let me send you back to Figure I.1 in the Introduction. What is next on the profession agenda? Where do we go from here? The pricing profession is gaining traction slowly but surely. Is predictive analytics next? Is the Big Data phenomenon going to absorb pricing and merge it with sales and marketing analytics? What should the profession get ready for in the next 20 years? One thing is for sure: the speed of transformation of the pricing profession is going to accelerate. What used to take 30 or 40 years will now happen in a decade or less. Change is accelerating for the pricing discipline. Get on the change train!

The 5C model of pricing transformation, joining pricing capabilities and other organizational capabilities, is a first step to accelerate the transition to the organizational phase, as shown in Figure I.1. The more people read the need to focus on organizational and human capabilities, the more pricing is going to be deployed, assimilated, and absorbed in the firm's organizational fabrics. But this model needs further exploration. I have provided additional insights into the antecedents and consequences of organizational confidence. A similar quantitative approach may be needed for the role of champions and for the construct of organizational change capacity. I am certain that additional exploratory studies on these two constructs would strongly enrich and reinforce my overall argument. It would also provide practical recommendations regarding which dimensions of change and championing of pricing may accelerate the pricing journey. Understanding what influences or drives the capacity of an organization to change and embrace pricing is certainly needed. The goal is to identify additional organizational capabilities that may boost the adoption and assimilation of technical pricing resources and their related pricing activities and programs.

So far our research approach favored a parsimonious model. Although I conducted six surveys, more are needed to complete our overall theory. In fact, we may have missed some important organizational dimensions such as organizational agility, team collaboration, organizational culture, organizational learning, and organizational mindfulness. All these ideas may become relevant to explain more of the characteristics of organizational transformation in pricing. I hope to continue my research into this discipline, but I also invite emerging scholars to expand the exploration with me. Good theory is developed only through a process of inquiry, contradictory thesis, and constructive criticism. As a pricing evangelist, I hope to stimulate readers' minds at the same time as I engage the academic community.

Pricing can add value to any business. It is an important discipline that deserves a place at the table, whether the table in question belongs to marketing or the board of directors. The fact that it hasn't earned one yet at many companies is a managerial and not an intellectual failure. I hope this book will help correct that and trigger further interest in the field of pricing and in the development of more advanced concepts and theories. Much work has been done, but much more remains.

References

Anderson, J. C., D. C. Jain, and P. K. Chintagunta. 1993. "Customer Value Assessment in Business Markets: A State-of-Practice Study." *Journal of Business-to-Business Marketing* 1 (1): 3.

Anderson, J. C., N. Kumar, and J. A. Narus. 2007. *Value Merchants: Demonstrating and Documenting Superior Value in Business Markets.* Boston: Harvard Business School Press.

Anderson, J. C., and J. A. Narus. 1998. "Business Marketing: Understand What Customers Value." *Harvard Business Review* 76 (6): 53–65.

Anderson, J. C., M. Wouters, and W. van Rossum. 2010. "Why the Highest Price Isn't the Best Price." *MIT Sloan Management Review* 51 (2): 69–76.

Argyres, N. S., and B. S. Silverman. 2004. "R&D, Organization Structure, and the Development of Corporate Technological Knowledge." *Strategic Management Journal* 25 (8–9): 929–958.

Backman, J. 1953. *Pricing Practices and Policies: Rate Policies and Rate Practices of the United States Post Office.* New York: Ronald Press.

Bandura, A. 1986. *Social Foundations of Thought and Action: A Social Cognitive Theory.* Englewood Cliffs, NJ: Prentice-Hall.

———. 1997. *Self-Efficacy: The Exercise of Control.* New York: Freeman.

Barnard, C. I., and K. R. Andrews. 1968. *The Functions of the Executive.* Cambridge, MA: Harvard University Press.

Barney, J. B. 1991. "Firm Resources and Sustained Competitive Advantage." *Journal of Management* 17 (1): 99–120.

Berggren, K., and M. Eek. 2007. *The Emerging Pricing Capability.* Master's thesis, School of Economics and Management, Lund University.

Birkinshaw, J., and C. Gibson. 2004. "Building Ambidexterity into an Organization." *MIT Sloan Management Review* 45: 47–55.

Birkinshaw, J., and S. Heywood. 2010. "Putting Organizational Complexity in Its Place." *McKinsey Quarterly* (May): 1–9.

Bohn, J. G. 2001. "The Design and Validation of an Instrument to Assess Organizational Efficacy." Unpublished dissertation, University of Wisconsin–Milwaukee.

————. 2002. "The Relationship of Perceived Leadership Behaviors to Organizational Efficacy." *Journal of Leadership and Organizational Studies* 9 (2): 65–79.

Boyatzis, R. E. 2006. "An Overview of Intentional Change from a Complexity Perspective." *Journal of Management Development* 25 (7): 607–623.

Boyatzis, R. E., and A. McKee. 2005. *Resonant Leadership*. Boston: Harvard Business School Press.

Brandenburger, A. M., and H. W. Stuart. 1996. "Value-Based Business Strategy." *Journal of Economics and Management Strategy* 5: 5–24.

Brownlie, D., and J. C. Spender. 1995. "Managerial Judgement in Strategic Marketing." *Management Decision* 33 (6): 39–50.

Burke, L. A., and M. K. Miller. 1999. "Taking the Mystery out of Intuitive Decision Making." *Academy of Management Executive (1993–2005)* 13 (4): 91–99.

Butler, M. J. R. 2003. "Managing from the Inside Out: Drawing on 'Receptivity' to Explain Variation in Strategy Implementation." *British Journal of Management* 14: S47–S60.

Campbell, A., S. Kunisch, and G. Muller-Stewens. 2011. "To Centralize or Not to Centralize." *McKinsey Quarterly* (June).

Chakrabarti, A. K. 1974. "The Role of Champion in Product Innovation." *California Management Review* 17 (2): 58–62.

Chandler, A. D. 1973. *Strategy and Structure*. Cambridge, MA: MIT Press.

Cherns, A. B. 1976. "The Principles of Sociotechnical Design." *Human Relations* 29 (8): 783–792.

Cohen, W. M., and D. A. Levinthal. 1990. "Absorptive Capacity: A New Perspective on Learning and Innovation." *Administrative Science Quarterly* 35 (1).

Cressman, G. E., Jr. 1999. "Commentary on 'Industrial Pricing: Theory and Managerial Practice.'" *Marketing Science* 18 (3): 455–457.

Cummings, S. 1995. "Centralization and Decentralization: The Never Ending Story of Separation and Betrayal." *Scandinavian Journal of Management* 11 (2): 103–117.

Cyert, R. M., and J. G. March. 1992. *A Behavioral Theory of the Firm*. Cambridge, MA: Wiley-Blackwell.

Daft, R. L., and N. B. Macintosh. 1981. "A Tentative Exploration into the Amount and Equivocality of Information Processing in Organizational Work Units." *Administrative Science Quarterly* 26 (2): 207–224.

Daft, R. L., and K. E. Weick. 1984. "Toward a Model of Organizations as Interpretation Systems." *Academy of Management Review* 9 (2): 284–295.

Dalton, M. 1959. *Men Who Manage*. New York: Wiley.

Dane, E., and M. G. Pratt. 2007. "Exploring Intuition and Its Role in Managerial Decision Making." *Academy of Management Review* 32 (1): 33.

Day, G. S. 1994. "The Capabilities of Market-Driven Organizations." *Journal of Marketing* 58 (4): 37–52.

Dierickx, I., and K. Cool. 1989. "Asset Stock Accumulation and Sustainability of Competitive Advantage." *Management Science* 35 (12): 1504–1511.

Dillman, D. A., J. D. Smyth, and L. M. Christian. 2009. "Internet, Mail, and Mixed-Mode Surveys: The Tailored Design Method." In *Internet, Mail and Mixed-Mode Surveys: The Tailored Design Method*, 3rd ed., edited by D. Dillman and B. Groves. Hoboken, NJ: Wiley, 2009.

DiMaggio, P. J., and W. W. Powell. 1983. "The Iron Cage Revisited: Institutional Isomorphism and Collective Rationality in Organizational Fields." *American Sociological Review* 48 (2): 147–160.

Doherty, N. F., and M. King. 2005. "From Technical to Socio-Technical Change: Tackling the Human and Organizational Aspects of Systems Development Projects." *European Journal of Information Systems* 14 (1): 1–5.

Dolan, R. J. 1995. "How Do You Know When the Price Is Right?" *Harvard Business Review* 73 (5): 174–183.

Dolan, R. J., and H. Simon. 1996. *Power Pricing: How Managing Price Transforms the Bottom Line*. New York: Free Press.

Duncan, R. B. 1972. "Characteristics of Organizational Environments and Perceived Environmental Uncertainty." *Administrative Science Quarterly* 17 (3): 313–327.

Dutta, S., M. E. Bergen, D. Levy, M. Ritson, and M. Zbaracki. 2002. "Pricing as a Strategic Capability." *MIT Sloan Management Review* 43 (3): 61–66.

Dutta, S., M. J. Zbaracki, and M. Bergen. 2003. "Pricing Process as a Capability: A Resource-Based Perspective." *Strategic Management Journal* 24 (7): 615–630. doi:10.1002/smj.323.

Duymedjian, R., and C. C. Rüling. 2010. "Towards a Foundation of Bricolage in Organization and Management Theory." *Organization Studies* 31 (2): 133.

Evaristo, J. R., K. C. Desouza, and K. Hollister. 2005. "Centralization Momentum: The Pendulum Swings Back Again." *Communications of the ACM* 48 (2): 66–71.

Fayol, H. 1949. *General and Industrial Administration*. London: Pitman.

Feldman, M. S. 2000. "Organizational Routines as a Source of Continuous Change." *Organization Science* 11 (6): 611–629.

Fiol, C. M., and E. J. O'Connor. 2003. "Waking Up! Mindfulness in the Face of Bandwagons." *Academy of Management Review* 28 (1): 54–70.

Forbis, J. L., and N. T. Mehta. 1981. "Value-Based Strategies for Industrial Products." *Business Horizons* 24 (3): 32–42.

Fredrickson, B. 2009. *Positivity: Groundbreaking Research Reveals How to Embrace the Hidden Strength of Positive Emotions, Overcome Negativity, and Thrive*. New York: Crown.

Frenzen, H., A. K. Hansen, M. Krafft, M. K. Mantrala, and S. Schmidt. 2010. "Delegation of Pricing Authority to the Sales Force: An Agency-Theoretic Perspective of Its Determinants and Impact on Performance." *International Journal of Research in Marketing* 27 (1): 58–68.

Frye, A., and D. Campbell. 2011. "Buffett Says Pricing Power More Important Than Good Management." Bloomberg.com, February 18.

Geels, F. W. 2004. "From Sectoral Systems of Innovation to Socio-Technical Systems: Insights About Dynamics and Change from Sociology and Institutional Theory." *Research Policy* 33 (6): 897–920.

Graf, L., A. König, A. Enders, and H. Hungenberg. 2012. "Debiasing Competitive Irrationality: How Managers Can Be Prevented from Trading Off Absolute for Relative Profit." *European Management Journal* 30 (4): 386–403.

Green, S. G., and T. D. Taber. 1978. "Structuring Experiential Learning Through Experimentation." *Academy of Management Review* 3 (4): 889–895.

Gully, S. M., K. A. Incalcaterra, A. Joshi, and J. M. Beaubien. 2002. "A Meta-Analysis of Team-Efficacy, Potency, and Performance: Interdependence and Level of Analysis as Moderators of Observed Relationships." *Journal of Applied Psychology* 87 (5): 819–832.

Hall, R. H. 1977. *Organization, Structure, and Process*. Vol. 2. London: Prentice-Hall.

Hallberg, N. 2008. *Pricing Capability and Its Strategic Dimensions*. PhD thesis, School of Economics and Management, Lund University.

Hambrick, D. C., M. A. Geletkanycz, and J. W. Fredrickson. 1993. "Top Executive Commitment to the Status Quo: Some Tests of Its Determinants." *Strategic Management Journal* 14 (6): 401–418.

Hinterhuber, A. 2004. "Towards Value-Based Pricing—An Integrative Framework for Decision Making." *Industrial Marketing Management* 33 (8): 765–778. doi: 10.1016/j.indmarman.2003.10.006.

———. 2008a. "Customer Value-Based Pricing Strategies: Why Companies Resist." *Journal of Business Strategy* 29 (4): 41–50.

———. 2008b. "Value Delivery and Value-Based Pricing in Industrial Markets." *Advances in Business Marketing and Purchasing* 14: 381–448.

Hinterhuber, A., and S. Liozu. 2012. "Is It Time to Rethink Your Pricing Strategy?" *MIT Sloan Management Review* 53 (4): 69–77.

Holt, D. T., A. A. Armenakis, H. S. Feild, and S. G. Harris. 2007. "Readiness for Organizational Change." *Journal of Applied Behavioral Science* 43 (2): 232.

Hoover, J., and A. Valenti. 2005. *Unleashing Leadership: Aligning What People Do Best with What Organizations Need Most*. Franklin Lakes, NJ: Career Press.

Howell, J. M., and C. A. Higgins. 1990. "Champions of Technological Innovation." *Administrative Science Quarterly* 35 (2): 317–341.

Howell, J. M., C. M. Shea, and C. A. Higgins. 2005. "Champions of Product Innovations: Defining, Developing, and Validating a Measure of Champion Behavior." *Journal of Business Venturing* 20 (5): 641–661.

Hunt, P., and J. Saunders. 2013. *World Class Pricing: The Journey*. Bloomington, IN: iUniverse.

Ingenbleek, P. 2007. "Value-Informed Pricing in Its Organizational Context: Literature Review, Conceptual Framework, and Directions for Future Research." *Journal of Product and Brand Management* 16 (7): 441–458. doi: 10.1108/10610420710834904.

Ingenbleek, P., M. Debruyne, R. T. Frambach, and T. M. M. Verhallen. 2001. "On Cost-Informed Pricing and Customer Value: A Resource-Advantage Perspective on Industrial Innovation Pricing Practices." University Park, PA: Pennsylvania State University, Institute for the Study of Business Markets.

———. 2003. "Successful New Product Pricing Practices: A Contingency Approach." *Marketing Letters* 14 (4): 289–305.

Judge, W. Q., and C. P. Blocker. 2008. "Organizational Capacity for Change and Strategic Ambidexterity: Flying the Plane While Rewiring It." *European Journal of Marketing* 42 (9–10): 915–926.

Judge, W., and T. Douglas. 2009. "Organizational Change Capacity: The Systematic Development of a Scale." *Journal of Organizational Change Management* 22 (6): 635–649.

Kanter, R. M. 1984. *The Change Masters: Innovation and Entrepreneurship in the American Corporation*. New York: Simon and Schuster.

———. 2006. *Confidence: How Winning Streaks and Losing Streaks Begin and End*. New York: Three Rivers Press.

Kerlinger, F. N., and Lee, H. B. 1999. *Foundations of Behavioral Research*. Fort Worth, TX: Harcourt College Publishers.

Khatri, N., and H. A. Ng. 2000. "The Role of Intuition in Strategic Decision Making." *Human Relations* 53 (1): 57.

Kolb, D. A. 1984. *Experiential Learning*. Englewood Cliffs, NJ: Prentice-Hall.

Kolb, D. A., R. E. Boyatzis, and C. Mainemelis. 2001. *Experiential Learning Theory: Previous Research and New Directions, Perspectives on Thinking, Learning, and Cognitive Styles*. Mahwah, NJ: Erlbaum.

Lancioni, R. 2005. "Pricing Issues in Industrial Marketing." *Industrial Marketing Management* 34 (2): 111–114. doi: 10.1016/j.indmarman.2004.07.009.

Lancioni, R., H. J. Schau, and M. F. Smith. 2005. "Intraorganizational Influences on Business-to-Business Pricing Strategies: A Political Economy Perspective." *Industrial Marketing Management* 34 (2): 123–131. doi: 10.1016/j.indmarman.2004.07.010.

Langer, E. J. 1989. *Mindfulness*. Reading, MA: Addison-Wesley.

————. 1997. *The Power of Mindful Learning*. Reading, MA: Addison-Wesley.

Leavitt, H. J. 1964. "Applied Organization Change in Industry: Structural, Technical and Human Approaches." In *New Perspectives in Organizational Research*, edited by S. Cooper, H. Leavitt, and K. Shelly, 55–71. Chichester, UK: Wiley.

Leonard-Barton, D. 1992. "Core Capabilities and Core Rigidities: A Paradox in Managing New Product Development." *Strategic Management Journal* 13 (S1): 111–125.

Leszinski, R., and M. V. Marn. 1997. "Setting Value, Not Price." *McKinsey Quarterly* (1): 98–115.

Lewicki, R. J., S. E. Weiss, and D. Lewin. 1992. "Models of Conflict, Negotiation and Third Party Intervention: A Review and Synthesis." *Journal of Organizational Behavior* 13 (3): 209–252.

Liozu, S. M. 2011. "Facing Commodity Price Bullies." *Journal of Professional Pricing* Q4: 8–11.

————. 2012. "Complexity Theory and Pricing Management." *Journal of Professional Pricing* Q3: 10–17.

————. 2014. "Change Management and Pricing." *Pricing Advisor* (February): 6–10.

Liozu, S. M., R. J. Boland, Jr., A. Hinterhuber, and S. Perelli. 2011. "Industrial Pricing Orientation: The Organizational Transformation to Value-Based Pricing." Paper presented at the International Conference on Engaged Management Scholarship, Case Western Reserve University, Cleveland, OH, June.

Liozu, S. M., and K. Ecker. 2012. "The Organizational Design of the Pricing Function in Firms." In *Innovation in Pricing: Contemporary Theories and Best Practices*, 27–45. New York: Routledge.

Liozu, S. M., and A. Hinterhuber. 2011. "The Pricing Function in Industrial Markets." *Journal of Professional Pricing* Q1: 20–24.

————. 2012a. "CEO Championing of Pricing, Pricing Capabilities and Firm Performance in Industrial Firms." *Industrial Marketing Management* 42: 633–643.

————. 2012b. "Industrial Product Pricing: A Value-Based Approach." *Journal of Business Strategy* 33 (4): 28–39.

————. 2013. "Pricing Orientation, Pricing Capabilities, and Firm Performance." *Management Decision* 51 (3): 594–614.

Liozu, S. M., A. Hinterhuber, R. Boland, and S. Perelli. 2012. "The Conceptualization of Value-Based Pricing in Industrial Firms." *Journal of Revenue and Pricing Management* 11 (1): 12–34.

Liozu, S. M., A. Hinterhuber, S. Perelli, and R. Boland. 2012. "Mindful Pricing: Transforming Organizations Through Value-Based Pricing." *Journal of Strategic Marketing* 20 (3): 197–209.

Liozu, S. M., A. Hinterhuber, and T. M. Somers. 2014. "Organizational Design and Pricing Capabilities for Superior Firm Performance." *Management Decision* 52 (1): 54–78.

Luna-Reyes, L. F., J. Zhang, J. R. Gil-García, and A. M. Cresswell. 2005. "Information Systems Development as Emergent Socio-Technical Change: A Practice Approach." *European Journal of Information Systems* 14 (1): 93–105.

Lynn, M. L. 2005. "Organizational Buffering: Managing Boundaries and Cores." *Organization Studies* 26 (1): 37–61.

Lyytinen, K., and M. Newman. 2008. "Explaining Information Systems Change: A Punctuated Socio-Technical Change Model." *European Journal of Information Systems* 17 (6): 589–613.

Lyytinen, K., and D. Robey. 1999. "Learning Failure in Information Systems Development." *Information Systems Journal* 9 (2): 85–101.

Makadok, R. 2001. "Toward a Synthesis of the Resource Based and Dynamic Capability Views of Rent Creation." *Strategic Management Journal* 22 (5): 387–401.

March, J. G. 1978. "Bounded Rationality, Ambiguity, and the Engineering of Choice." *Bell Journal of Economics* 9 (2): 587–608.

March, J. G., H. A. Simon, and H. Guetzkow. 1958. *Organizations.* New York: Wiley.

Marn, M. V., E. V. Roegner, and C. C. Zawada. 2004. *The Price Advantage.* New York: Wiley.

Matthyssens, P., K. Vandenbempt, and L. Berghman. 2006. "Value Innovation in Business Markets: Breaking the Industry Recipe." *Industrial Marketing Management* 35 (6): 751–761. doi: 10.1016/j.indmarman.2005.05.013.

Meyer, C. B., and I. G. Stensaker. 2006. "Developing Capacity for Change." *Journal of Change Management* 6 (2): 217–231.

Mezirow, J. 1996. "Contemporary Paradigms of Learning." *Adult Education Quarterly* 46 (3): 158.

———. 2000. *Learning to Think Like an Adult—Learning as Transformation: Critical Perspectives on a Theory in Progress.* San Francisco: Jossey-Bass.

Miller, C. C., and R. D. Ireland. 2005. "Intuition in Strategic Decision Making: Friend or Foe in the Fast-Paced 21st Century?" *Academy of Management Executive* 19 (1): 19–30.

Miller, S. L. 2009. *Why Teams Win: 9 Keys to Success in Business, Sport and Beyond.* Mississauga, ON: Wiley.

Mitchell, K. 2011. "The Current State of Pricing Practice in U.S. Firms (Opening Speech)." Paper presented at the Professional Pricing Society Annual Spring Conference, Chicago.

———. 2012. "The Next Frontier of the Pricing Profession." In *Innovation in Pricing: Contemporary Theories and Best Practices,* 403–409. New York: Routledge.

Moilanen, R. 2005. "Diagnosing and Measuring Learning Organizations." *Learning Organization* 12 (1): 71–89.

Morgan, N. A., D. W. Vorhies, and C. H. Mason. 2009. "Market Orientation, Marketing Capabilities, and Firm Performance." *Strategic Management Journal* 30 (8): 909–920.

Mumford, E. 2006. "The Story of Socio technical Design: Reflections on Its Successes, Failures and Potential." *Information Systems Journal* 16 (4): 317–342.

Nadler, D. A. 1997. *Champions of Change: How CEOs and Their Companies Are Mastering the Skills of Radical Change*. San Francisco: Jossey-Bass.

Nadler, D. A., and M. L. Tushman. 1990. "Beyond the Charismatic Leader and Organizational Change." *California Management Review* (Winter): 77–97.

Nagle, T. T., and R. K. Holden. 2002. *The Strategy and Tactics of Pricing: A Guide to Profitable Decision Making*. Englewood Cliffs, NJ: Prentice-Hall.

Oxenfeldt, A. R. 1973. "A Decision-Making Structure for Price Decisions." *Journal of Marketing* 37 (1): 48–53.

Pentland, B. T., and H. H. Reuter. 1994. "Organizational Routines as Grammars of Action." *Administrative Science Quarterly* 39 (3): 484–510.

Pfeffer, J. 1994. *Managing with Power: Politics and Influence in Organizations*. Boston: Harvard Business School Press.

Pfeffer, J., and R. I. Sutton. 2006. "Evidence-Based Management." *Harvard Business Review* 84: 1–12.

Pondy, L. R. 1969. "Varieties of Organizational Conflict." *Administrative Science Quarterly*: 499–505.

———. 1992. "Overview of Organizational Conflict: Concepts and Models." *Journal of Organizational Behavior* 13 (3): 255–255.

Porac, J. F., H. Thomas, and C. Baden-Fuller. 1989. "Competitive Groups as Cognitive Communities: The Case of Scottish Knitwear Manufacturers." *Journal of Management Studies* 26 (4): 397–416.

Priem, R. L., and J. E. Butler. 2001. "Is the Resource-Based 'View' a Useful Perspective for Strategic Management Research?" *Academy of Management Review*: 22–40.

Schön, D. A. 1963. "Champions for Radical New Innovations." *Harvard Business Review* 41 (2): 77–86.

Schwenk, C. R. 1988. "The Cognitive Perspective on Strategic Decision Making." *Journal of Management Studies* 25 (1): 41–55.

Shipley, D., and E. Bourdon. 1990. "Distributor Pricing in Very Competitive Markets." *Industrial Marketing Management* 19 (4): 215–224.

Simon, H. A. 1961. *Administrative Behavior*. New York: Macmillan.

———. 1987. "Making Management Decisions: The Role of Intuition and Emotion." *Academy of Management Executive* 1 (1): 57–64.

Simon, H., H. Guetzkow, G. Kozmetsky, and G. Tyndall. 1954. *Centralization vs. Decentralization in Organizing the Controller's Department, Controllership Foundation Inc.* New York: Scholars Book Co.

Simon Kucher & Partners. 2011. Global Pricing Study.

———. 2012. Global Pricing Study.

Simsek, Z., C. Heavey, and J. J. F. Veiga. 2010. "The Impact of CEO Core Self Evaluation on the Firm's Entrepreneurial Orientation." *Strategic Management Journal* 31 (1): 110–119.

Smith, G. E., and T. T. Nagle. 2005. "A Question of Value." *Marketing Management* 14 (4): 38–43.

Sodhi, M. S., and N. S. Sodhi. 2005. "Six Sigma Pricing." *Harvard Business Review* 83 (5): 135–142.

Spender, J. C. 1989. *Industry Recipes*. Oxford: Basil Blackwell.

Steffens, P. R., J. M. Senyard, and T. Baker. 2009. "Linking Resource Acquisition and Development Processes to Resource-Based Advantage: Bricolage and the Resource-Based View." Paper presented at the AGSE International Entrepreneurship Research Exchange, University of Adelaide, Australia, February.

Szulanski, G. 1996. "Exploring Internal Stickiness: Impediments to the Transfer of Best Practices within the Firm." *Strategic Management Journal* 17: 27–43.

Tasa, K., S. Taggar, and G. H. Seijts. 2007. "The Development of Collective Efficacy in Teams: A Multilevel and Longitudinal Perspective." *Journal of Applied Psychology* 92 (1): 17–27.

Teece, D. J., G. Pisano, and A. Shuen. 1997. "Dynamic Capabilities and Strategic Management." *Strategic Management Journal* 18 (7): 509–533.

Thomke, S. H. 2003. *Experimentation Matters*. Boston: Harvard Business School Press.

Tushman, M. L., and T. J. Scanlan. 1981. "Characteristics and External Orientations of Boundary Spanning Individuals." *Academy of Management Journal* 24 (1): 83–98.

Van de Ven, A. H. 2007. *Engaged Scholarship: A Guide for Organizational and Social Research*. New York: Oxford University Press.

Vorhies, D. W., and N. A. Morgan. 2005. "Benchmarking Marketing Capabilities for Sustainable Competitive Advantage." *Journal of Marketing* 69 (1): 80–94.

Walsh, J. P., and G. R. Ungson. 1991. "Organizational Memory." *Academy of Management Review* 16 (1): 57–91.

Weick, K. E., and K. M. Sutcliffe. 2007. *Managing the Unexpected: Resilient Performance in an Age of Uncertainty*. San Francisco: Jossey-Bass.

Weick, K. E., K. M. Sutcliffe, and D. Obstfeld. 1999. "Organizing for High Reliability: Processes of Collective Mindfulness." *Research in Organizational Behavior* 21: 81–123.

Yuksel, U., and C. Sutton-Brady. 2011. "To Delegate or Not To Delegate? That Is the Question of Pricing Authority." *Journal of Business and Economics Research (Since 2003)* 4 (2): 35–44.

Zahra, S. A., and G. George. 2002. "Absorptive Capacity: A Review, Reconceptualization, and Extension." *Academy of Management Review* 27 (2): 185–203.

Index